Poems of Love and War

Translations from the Oriental Classics

POEMS OF LOVE AND WAR

from the Eight Anthologies
and the Ten Long Poems
of Classical Tamil

selected and translated
by

A. K. Ramanujan

New York -- Columbia University Press

UNESCO COLLECTION OF REPRESENTATIVE WORKS

Indian Series

This book, translated from the Tamil, has been accepted in the translations collection of the United Nations Educational, Scientific and Cultural Organization (UNESCO)

Library of Congress Cataloging in Publication Data

Main entry under title:

Poems of love and war, from the eight anthologies
and the ten long poems of classical Tamil.
(Translations based on: Eṭṭuttokai, Pattuppāṭṭu;
and Tolkāppiyam.)
Bibliography: p.
1. Tamil poetry—To 1500—Translations into
English. 2. English poetry—Translations from
Tamil. I. Ramanujan, A. K., 1929–
II. Tolkāppiyar. Tolkāppiyam. English.
III. Eṭṭuttokai. English. IV. Pattuppāṭṭu.
English. V. Series.
PL4758.65.E5P63 1984 894′.81111′08 84-12182
ISBN 0-231-05106-9
ISBN 0-231-05107-7 (pbk.)

Columbia University Press
New York Chichester, West Sussex

Printed in the United States of America

c 10 9 8 7 6 5 4 3 2 1
p 10 9 8

Casebound editions of Columbia University Press books are printed on permanent and durable acid-free paper

for
Helen and Milton Singer

Contents

Translator's Note

Tamil, one of the two classical languages of India, is a Dravidian[1] language spoken today by 50 million Indians, mainly in Tamilnadu State (formerly Madras) in the southeast region of peninsular India. Tamil is also spoken in Sri Lanka, Malaysia, and the Fiji Islands.

In this book, *Poems of Love and War,* I attempt translations of old Tamil poems selected from anthologies compiled about two millennia ago. Today we have access to over two thousand of these poems composed by nearly 500 poets. These poems are "classical," i.e., early, ancient; they are also "classics," i.e., works that have stood the test of time, the founding works of a whole tradition. Not to know them is not to know a unique and major poetic achievement of Indian civilization.

The Texts

Early classical Tamil literature (c. 100 B.C.–A.D. 250) consists of the Eight Anthologies *(Eṭṭuttokai),* the Ten Long Poems *(Pattuppāṭṭu),*[2] and a grammar called the *Tolkāppi-*

yam or the "Old Composition."[3] The poems in this book are selected from the Eight Anthologies and the Ten Long Poems; sections of the *Tolkāppiyam* are used to develop a commentary on Tamil poetry and poetics. Apart from some epigraphic and archaeological evidence, the classical literature is the most important native source of historical and cultural information for this period in Tamil South India.[4]

The literature of classical Tamil later came to be known as *Caṅkam* (pronounced *Sangam*) literature. The word does not occur in the poems. *Caṅkam* means "an academy or fraternity"; a seventh-century commentator applied the term to poetry and spoke of three academies or Caṅkams, lasting 4,440, 3,700, and 1,850[5] years respectively, with a membership of gods, sages, and kings as poets. A whole mythology grew around the poems and poets; especially popular is the myth of a Great Flood that destroyed millennia-old kingdoms and a large body of literature. Such myths certainly point to a long poetic tradition, with much of it lost in the great flood of time. All the works of the first Caṅkam are said to be lost; only the grammar *Tolkāppiyam* remains of the second; the Eight Anthologies and the Ten Long Poems belong to the third.

The Poems and the Poets

Caṅkam poems vary in length from 3 to over 800 lines. There are 2,381 Caṅkam poems, of which 102 are anonymous (Vaiyāpuri Piḷḷai 1940). Nearly half the poems were composed by no more than 16 poets, though 473 poets are known by proper names or by epithets. The largest number assigned to any poet is 235, to Kapilar; next to him stands Ammūvaṉar with 127 poems. Five poets are represented by over 100 poems; 293 poets are represented by a single poem.

Many poets are named after a striking phrase or metaphor in the poems assigned to them. For instance, the following poem, *Kuṟuntokai* 40, is by Cempulappeyaṉīrār, which would mean "The Poet of the Red Earth and Pouring Rain."

What He Said

What could my mother be
to yours? What kin is my father
to yours anyway? And how
did you and I meet ever?
                    But in love
our hearts have mingled
like red earth and pouring rain.

Similarly, *Kuṟuntokai* 370 (p. 102) is by Villakaviraliṉār, "The Poet of the Fingers Around the Bow." Poets were known by their poems. Their metaphors were their signatures.

A Tradition Lost and Found

These classics were not always known to the Tamils themselves. They were dramatically rediscovered in the later decades of the nineteenth century, a period of transition, when both paper and palm leaf were used as writing materials. The great texts of classical Tamil literature, including the Eight Anthologies and the Twin Epics *(Cilappatikāram* and *Maṇimēkalai)* were inaccessible to most scholars all through the early nineteenth century, though they were known and had been commented on a century earlier. Eighteenth-century Hindu scholars, devout worshipers of Śiva or Viṣṇu, had tabooed as irreligious all secular and non-Hindu texts, which included the classical Tamil anthologies. They also disallowed the study of Jain and Buddhist texts, which included the Twin Epics. Under this restriction and taboo, even the finest of Tamil scholars, such as Cāmināta Aiyar (who is the hero of this section), had to give their days and nights of impassioned study to the religious and grammatical texts of the medieval period, many of which were of minor importance.

Cāmināta Aiyar (1855–1942), a man of vast learning, was entirely unaware even of the existence of the breathtaking epics and anthologies of early Tamil, until he met a liberal-minded *munsif* (civil judge) named Rāmacuvāmi Mutaliyār, in a small temple town, Kumpakōṇam. Aiyar records the date of this fateful meeting, for it was no less, as October 21, 1880, a Thursday. To him, as to all students of Tamil literature, this date is "etched in red letters." The *munsif* had just been transferred to that small town. When Aiyar met him, the judge asked him what he had studied and under whom. Aiyar named his well-known mentor and listed all the grammars, religious texts, and commentaries he had labored over. The judge, unimpressed, asked him, "That's all? What use is that? Have you studied the old texts?" He named some. Aiyar, one of the most erudite and thoroughgoing of Tamil scholars, was aghast that he had not even heard of them. The judge then gave him a handwritten manuscript to take home and read. In his autobiography (the chapter is called "What Is the Use?"), Aiyar says the good fortune of his past lives took him there that Thursday and opened a new life for him. Cāmināta Aiyar, who was 44 then, devoted the rest of his long life to roaming the villages, rummaging in private attics and the storerooms of monasteries, to unearthing, editing, and printing classical Tamil texts (Cāminātaiyar 1952: 326–43).

It is to him and to his peers, such as Ci. Vay. Tāmōtaram Piḷḷai (1832–1901), that we owe our knowledge of this major tradition. They rescued manuscripts from oblivion and put them into print and circulation. Piḷḷai described the situation in the late nineteenth century in a preface he wrote to the first edition (1877) of one of the Eight Anthologies:

> Only what has escaped fire and water [and religious taboo] remains; even of that, termites and the bug named Rama's Arrow take a toll; the third element, earth, has its share. . . . When you untie a knot, the leaf cracks. When you turn a leaf, it breaks in half. . . . Old manuscripts are crumbling and there is no one to make new copies.

Even when they were available, the manuscripts had many errors and interpolations. Texts differed greatly from copy to copy. (The work of rigorous modern textual criticism has barely begun.) Only some scholars and some sectarian monasteries protected the texts they liked and revered. Each community studied its own texts. If, for some reason, a Śaivite scribe copied a Jain text, important emendations were likely to be made. A few kings and rich men arranged for copies to be made when the old manuscripts fell apart. The scribes had to be well chosen and well paid. If someone wished to read a book, he had to go in search of it. Manuscript owners did not lend them out, for good reason. They were guarded like treasures and passed from generation to generation in the family like heirlooms until some ignoramus threw one as a peace offering to angry floods or lighted the kitchen fires with it.

One reason for the complete absence of Buddhist manuscripts in the Tamil area (with one famous exception, *Maṇimēkalai*), is that no one preserved them or copied them after the Hindu Śaivites and Vaiṣṇavites triumphed over Buddhism. Jain manuscripts survived very well, because of a ritual practice called *śāstradānam* observed by the rich: the ritual called for giving new copies of old religious manuscripts to scholars on occasions like weddings. Regarding the expense, the Christian scholar Rev. P. Percival said that he bought a palm leaf manuscript for ten pounds before 1835; when it was printed later, he could get it for two and a half shillings.

Written texts, and among them the very classics that are the pride of Tamils today, were thus precariously, expensively, often only accidentally, transmitted. The story of Cāmināta Aiyar dramatizes the transition from palm leaf to print, from a period of private sectarian ownership of texts to a period of free access to them (Ramanujan 1970a).

This Book

In the rhetoric, and in the anthologies, the poems were classified by their themes as *akam* and *puṟam*. *Akam* (pronounced *aham*) meant "interior," *puṟam* "exterior." *Akam* poems were love poems; *puṟam* poems were poems on war, kings, death, etc. The two types of poems had differing properties. Three hundred and seven poets composed only the former, 89 only the latter, though 77 poets, including five of the greatest, wrote both kinds of poems.

The selections here, accordingly, have one book of *akam* poems and one of *puṟam*. The *akam* poems are presented in five sections, as they are in several of the anthologies. Each section contains poems that evoke a particular landscape: hillside, seaside, forests, cultivated fields, and the wilderness (or desert). Each landscape, with the mood it represents and the poems that evoke it, is called by the name of a flower or plant of that region: *kuṟiñci*, a mountain flower; *neytal*, blue lily; *mullai*, jasmine; *marutam*, queen's-flower; *pālai*, a desert tree.

Puṟam poems are not arranged according to landscapes in the anthologies, though such a classification is often implied. As foci for poems, certain situations (e.g., a siege), persons (e.g., a chieftain), and themes (e.g., ideals of the good life) seem to be more important than the landscapes. So I have arranged these poems under five themes: Kings at War, Poets and Dancers, Chieftains, Lessons, War and After.

The third and fourth books consist of a small sample of late classical poems (c. fifth to sixth century), poems in a different key. The third offers some comic, earthy, even bawdy poems, poems of love's excess in contrast to the decorum of the previous sections. It also includes an unusual poem on the bull fight contests of the time. The fourth and last book includes a long hymn to Viṣṇu, one of the earliest examples of its kind in Indian literature, and two pieces from the long poem, "A Guide to Lord Murukaṉ" (*Tirumurukāṟṟuppaṭai*). The erotic and heroic motifs of *akam* and *puṟam* are imaginatively reworked in these early, important, religious poems. Gods like Kṛṣṇa and Murukaṉ, who appear earlier in Tamil poetry than anywhere else, appear as gods of love and war. In these poems of praise addressed to them, we see classicism transformed into bhakti, a new kind of Hinduism.

The poems are followed by an afterword (a way of saying the poetry comes first): an essay on the Tamil world picture and its relation to Tamil poetry and poetics. Notes and indexes end the book.

The transliteration of Tamil words follows the Tamil Lexicon.

Acknowledgments

I began this book of translations fifteen years ago and thought several times that I had finished it. Translations too, being poems, are "never finished, only abandoned" (Valéry).

Over these fifteen years, as I accumulated these poems, I have also accumulated debts—beginning at home with my late mother who gave me more than a mother tongue, and my wife Molly whose literary insight and advice have been a mainstay, and not ending with the Tamil scholars past and present, and fellow workers in different parts of the world, such as Kamil Zvelebil, K. Kailasapathy, and George Hart. The latest of these debts is to two colleagues, Rajam Ramamurthy (University of Pennsylvania) and Keith Harrison (Carleton College). Rajam checked every one of these poems against her deep and meticulous knowledge of the Tamil texts, offered many suggestions, corrected many errors. Keith Harrison, poet and translator, read them all in more than one version, and tested every nut and bolt of this craft as he would his own boat before he goes sailing. He acted as a second poetic conscience that often spoke more clearly than my own. If the poems still have errors and awkwardnesses, as I am sure they do, it is because I did not always listen to their expert advice. The notes and queries of Barbara Stoler Miller, James Lindholm, Norman Cutler, Paula Richman, Vinay Dharwadker, and Robert Tisdale were helpful in reworking these pages. I thank them all.

At the University of Chicago, my two chairmen, Edward C. Dimock, Jr. and Paul Wheatley, and Dean Karl Weintraub have been infinitely helpful in difficult moments, and they supported me even on ordinary days. Their friendship, as that of colleagues in the Department of South Asian Languages and the Committee on Social Thought (especially of Wendy O'Flaherty and David Grene), has been a source of pleasure, ideas, energy. I worked on the last drafts in a third-floor office of the Department of English at Carleton College where I sat unsociably day after day agonizing over Tamil particles and English prepositions. I wish to thank my colleagues at Carleton College, as well as President Robert Edwards and Dean Peter Stanley, for their longstanding friendship in a place of haunting beauty, especially during the summer and fall of 1982.

Even one's own tradition is not one's birthright; it has to be earned, repossessed. The old bards earned it by apprenticing themselves to the masters. One chooses and translates a part of one's past to make it present to oneself and maybe to others. One comes face to face with it sometimes in faraway places, as I did. In 1962, on one of my first Saturdays at the University of Chicago, I entered the basement stacks of the then Harper Library in search of an elementary grammar of Old Tamil, which I had never learned. The University had just acquired a large collection of books from a famous South Indian historian. It was still uncatalogued, even undusted. As I searched, hoping to find a school grammar, I came upon an early anthology of classical Tamil poems, edited in 1937 by U. Vē. Cāminātaiyar. It carried his Tamil signature, dated 1937, on its flyleaf. That edition, I later learned, was a landmark in its own right. I sat down on the floor between the stacks and began to browse. To my amazement, I found the prose commentary transparent; it soon unlocked the old poems for me. As I began to read on, I was enthralled by the beauty and subtlety of what I could read. Here was a world, a part of my language and culture, to which I had been an ignorant heir. Until then, I had only heard of the idiot in the Bible who had gone looking for a donkey and had happened upon a kingdom.

That collection of Tamil books was there thanks to Milton Singer and his colleagues, who had decided to bring South Asia to Chicago. It is but fitting that I should dedicate this book of Tamil poems to Helen Singer, poet and friend of poets, and to Milton Singer, anthropologist and man of vision. I count their presence and friendship among my blessings.

Dancers and composers have translated my translations further into their own arts. Over the years, the poems have appeared not only in a variety of anthologies but in wedding services. The ancient poets composed in Tamil for their Tamil corner of the world of antiquity; but, as nothing human is alien, they have reached ages unborn and "accents yet unknown." I am grateful, and astonished, to be one of the links, undreamed of by them or by me.

A. K. Ramanujan

THE POEMS

BOOK ONE

Akam Poems

Kuṟiñci, the hills:	Lovers' Meetings
Neytal, the seashore:	Anxious Waiting and Secret Meetings
Pālai, the wasteland:	The Lovers' Journey Through the Wilderness
Mullai, the forest:	Patient Waiting and Happiness in Marriage
Marutam, the lowland:	The Lover's Unfaithfulness After Marriage

The selections in this section are from four anthologies:

Kuṟuntokai

Naṟṟiṇai

Akanāṉūṟu

Aiṅkuṟunūṟu

KUṞIÑCI: LOVERS' MEETINGS

What She Said

Bigger than earth, certainly,
higher than the sky,
more unfathomable than the waters
is this love for this man

of the mountain slopes
where bees make rich honey
from the flowers of the kuṟiñci
that has such black stalks.

Tēvakulattār
Kuṟuntokai 3

What She Said
to her girl friend

In his country,

summer west wind blows
flute music
through bright beetle-holes in the waving bamboos.
The sweet sound of waterfalls is continuous,
dense as drums.
The urgent lowing voices of a herd of stags
are oboes,
the bees on the flowering slopes
become lutes.

Excited by such teeming voices,
an audience of female monkeys
watches in wonder
the peacock in the bamboo hill
sway and strut
like a dancer
making an entrance
on a festival stage.

He had a garland on his chest,
a strong bow in his grip,
arrow already chosen,
and he asked which way
the elephant went
with an arrow buried in its side.

He stood at the edge
of a ripe-eared millet field.

But, among all the people
who saw him standing there,
why is it
that I alone

lie in bed
in this harsh night,
eyes streaming,
arms growing lean?

Kapil̲ar
Akanāṉūṟu 82

Ten on Lovers' Meetings

What She Said
to her girl friend, her foster-mother within earshot

Bless you. Listen to me:

my man wore the flowers,
  and there were young leaves for me;

their blossoms gold,
  their buds, sapphire;

tell me, what do you call
those trees on his mountain slopes?

What She Said

And all those horses
our man of the tall hills
comes riding on

    have tufts of hair
    like the brahman urchins
    in our town.

What She Said

to her girl friend,
when she returned from the hills

Bless you, friend. Listen.

Sweeter than milk
mixed with honey from our gardens

is the leftover water in his land,

low in the waterholes
covered with leaves

and muddied by animals.

What She Said

her lover within earshot

Tell me:
how is it then
that women gather
like hill goddesses

and stare at me
wherever I go,
and say
"She's good, she's so good,"

and I,
no good at all for my man
from the country of the hills?

What the Girl Friend Said
to the foster-mother

Listen.

My friend,
usually modest,
so fearful even of you, Mother,
will only sleep now
on the broad chest
of that man
from the tall hills
with their crashing white waterfalls:

and it hurts
to look at her.

What Her Friend Said

But look,

look at him out there

standing like a sentinel
who keeps a rain-tank from flooding,

        rain-wet bright sword
        hung at his side,
        war anklet
        twined with moss,
        his striped waist-cloth
        tight,
        and wet with dew.

What Her Friend Said

to her, before the rains

Is your crop of millet
parching?

Look, the raincloud sits
on the sapphire hills
of your man

like fat
on a cut of meat.

What Her Friend Said

to the foster-mother

Bless you, Mother, but listen.

Whenever the blue-stone hills
of his place

    where the hill tribes
    dig for tubers
    in long pits
    now filled with the new gold
    of kino flowers,

whenever those blue hills
fall from sight
each evening,

her long flower-like eyes
fill with tears.

What She Said
to her friend

You ask me to forget him,
how can I?

His mountain,
wearing its dark raincloud
white-crested

as a bean flower
the east wind opens,

his mountain,
that blue sapphire,
is never out of sight.

What Her Friend Said
to the foster-mother (who is guarding her carefully)

Bless you, Mother, listen.

She climbs the round garden rock
that reeks
of the meat of sacrifice,

she looks at the flowering hilltops
of his country,

and she stands there forever
in her sapphire jewels:

only in this way
will her sickness
find its remedy.

Kapilar
Aiṅkuṟunūṟu 201–210

What She Said

Forest animals walk there
and elephants roam.
In the sky's high places
thunder rumbles.
But you come alone
in the night
along the narrow paths
of snakes and tigers,

O man of the mountain country,

　　that country of fruitful hills,
　　ancient conquests,
　　and wide spaces,
　　where the music of waterfalls
　　mingles with bee sounds
　　as drums with lute-strings.

If you wish to marry me, you can.
But one thing: do not come
along those narrow paths;

though, if you must, please,
when you leave here
and reach your village in the hills,
think of us
living in anxiety here,
and get that long horn you use
to signal your hounds
and hunters
straying in the bamboo jungle,

and blow on it
a little.

Kapilar
Akanāṉūṟu 318

What She Said
to her girl friend

On the tall hill
where the short-stemmed nightshade quivers,

a squatting cripple
sights a honey hive
above,
points to the honey,
cups his hands,
and licks his fingers:

so too,
even if one's lover
doesn't love or care,
it still feels good
inside

just to see him
now and then.

Paraṇar
Kuṟuntokai 60

What He Said

As a little white snake
with lovely stripes on its young body
troubles the jungle elephant

this slip of a girl
her teeth like sprouts of new rice
her wrists stacked with bangles

troubles me.

Catti Nātaṉār
Kuṟuntokai 119

What She Said

Only the thief was there, no one else.
And if he should lie, what can I do?

There was only
a thin-legged heron standing
on legs yellow as millet stems
and looking
for lampreys
in the running water

when he took me.

Kapilar
Kuṟuntokai 25

What Her Friend Said,
criticizing him to give her strength

The drum-footed black elephant's calf,

its crown still soft,
runs and plays
with the gypsy woman's boys,
their bodies all tiny joints,
boys from the seaside
where liquor is plentiful;

is sweet one day
but devours their millet the next:

so too, his games and laughter
turn to hate.

Kuṟiyiṟaiyār
("The Poet of the Tiny Joints")
Kuṟuntokai 394

What She Said

What will happen now?

The ripe, sweet, aromatic mangoes of summer
from the stout trees
in the yards
and the glowing inner segments
of green-skinned jackfruit,
mixed with honey,

age in long bottles,
        sections of the swaying bamboo,
and brew into a liquor
as powerful, as quick
as a viper.

        The hillsmen
        offer it first to the mountain,
        sky peak and living god;
        soon get drunk on it,
        served by their women in leaf skirts,
        and forget to guard
        the millet fields on the slopes
        which elephants attack and ravage.

        Then they feel outraged,
        gather in councils,
        young men and old men
        gripping their bows,
        and search the hills
        for the rogue animals,

        in the country
        of my man.

Heart, so trustful
of his sweet and empty speeches,
what will happen to you
now?

Maturai Iḷampālāciriyaṉ Cēntaṉ Kūttaṉār
Akanāṉūṟu 348

What She Said

The bare root of the bean is pink
like the leg of a jungle hen,
and herds of deer attack its overripe pods.

For the harshness
of this season of morning dew
there is no cure

but the breast of my man.

Aḷḷūr Naṉmullai
Kuṟuntokai 68

What Her Girl Friend Said

to her

Their throats glittering like blue sapphire,
tail feathers splendid,
the peacocks gather
with sweet calls,
                    dancers
skilled in slow-beat rhythms.

But you don't play anymore
like those peacocks
with your girl friends
in the long deep streams,
wearing wreaths of blue lily
        with petals like eyes,
tresses flaring
as they dance.

Your heart is anxious,
you're lonely, stricken
with pallor.
Now, what shall I say to Mother
if she should notice changes
and ask for reasons?

I know,
our man from the mountain top

        where long silver waterfalls shiver
        in the wind
        like white banners
        borne high on elephants
        with trappings on their brow,

I know
he has brought you these pangs.

But what shall I say to Mother
if she asks?

Maturai Marutaṉiḷanākaṉār
Akanāṉūṟu 358

What His Friend Said,
teasing the man in love

Love, love,
they say.
Love
is no disease,
no evil goddess.

Come to think of it,
dear man
with those great shoulders,
love is very much like an old bull,

enjoys a good lick
of the young grass
on the slope
of an old backyard:

a fantasy feast,
that's what love is.

Miḷaipperuṅ Kantaṉ
Kuṟuntokai 204

What She Said

He is from those mountains

    where the little black-faced monkey,
    playing in the sun,
    rolls the wild peacock's eggs
    on the rocks.

Yes, his love is always good
as you say, my friend,

but only for those strong enough
to bear it,

who will not cry their eyes out
or think anything of it

when he leaves.

Kapilar
Kuṟuntokai 38

What Her Friend Said
to her, within the lover's hearing

So few, really
were the days
your lover crushed your garland
of mixed flowers
in his clasp.

But O the scandal!

It was far louder
than the clamor
of the Koṅkars flashing their blades

when Atikaṉ,
commander of the Pāṇṭiya,
that king of the golden armor,
fell
with his elephant
in the wide field of Vākai

where the only wild fowl
were owls.

Paraṇar
Kuṟuntokai 393

What She Said
to her friend

The colors on the elephant's body
shine, as he grazes
with his herd
on bamboo shoots,
breaking down branches;
then, in thirst,
he goes to a watering place,
kills a crouching tiger
poised for attack.
Pouring rains
clean the tusks, wash down the blood on their tips,
as he walks slowly along slopes
of jagged rock.
He's arrogant
after finishing off a vicious enemy,
and with six-legged bees making lute-music
over the juices of his lust
he mounts his female,
then goes to sleep
in our man's banana groves.

Friend,
comforting me once, you said lovingly,
"The man is just right
for your rank and nature."
Sweet words those, bless you,
they've come true:
garlands smell on him
like nectar to people who crave it,
his chest's embrace so tight
there's no place
even for the waist of a bee,

and love
is tireless still
as on the very first day.

Kapilar
Akanāṉūṟu 332

What Her Girl Friend Said
to him

Sir,
        not that we did not hear the noise
        you made trying to open the bolted doors,
        a robust bull elephant
        stirring in the night
        of everyone's sleep;

we did. But as we fluttered inside
like a peacock in the net,
crest broken, tail feathers flying,

our good mother held us close
in her innocence
thinking to quell our fears.

Kaṇṇaṉ
Kuṟuntokai 244

What She Said

Like moss on water
in the town's water tank:

the body's pallor
clears

as my lover touches
and touches,

and spreads again,
as he lets go,

as he lets go.

Paraṇar
Kuṟuntokai 399

NEYTAL: ANXIOUS WAITING AND SECRET MEETINGS BY THE SEASHORE

What Her Girl Friend Said
to him when he wanted to come by day

O man of the seashore

where old women
dry their wet streaming hair
and look like a flock
of herons in the bay,

when people said,
a chariot comes here often
splattering
the dark neytal *lilies*
near the bubbling backwaters,

Mother said at once,
"Don't go out."

Ammūvaṉār
Aiṅkuṟunūṟu 186

What Her Girl Friend Said
to him (on her behalf) when he came by daylight

Playing with friends one time
we pressed a ripe seed
into the white sand
and forgot about it
till it sprouted

and when we nursed it tenderly
pouring sweet milk with melted butter,
Mother said,
"It qualifies
as a sister to you, and it's much better
than you,"
praising this laurel tree.

So
we're embarrassed
to laugh with you here

O man of the seashore
with glittering waters
where white conch shells,
their spirals turning right,
sound like the soft music
of bards at a feast.

Yet, if you wish,
there's plenty of shade
elsewhere.

Anon.
Naṟṟiṇai 172

Three on Bangles

What She Said

Friend, his seas swell and roar
making conch shells whirl on the sands.
But fishermen ply their little wooden boats
unafraid of the cold lash of the waves.

Look, my bangles
slip loose as he leaves,
grow tight as he returns,

and they give me away.

What Her Girl Friend Said
to him

Your sands are furrowed
by the movements
of right-spiralled conches.
The glitter of their pearls
cuts the dark.

But, tell me,
are these any good,
these white bangles you've brought,
filed from the shells of that sea?

What He Said

My love whose bangles
glitter, jingle,
as she chases crabs,

suddenly stands shy,
head lowered,
hair hiding her face:

but only till the misery of evening
passes, when she'll give me
the full pleasure

of her breasts.

Ammūvaṉār
Aiṅkuṟunūṟu 192, 193, 197

What Her Girl Friend Said
to him

Near the salt pans
the clusters of *neytal* and blue lily
are closing for the day.
The sea restlessly
brings in the lapping tide,
the side-pincered crab
surfaces from its wet nest
of black clay,
and the seaside falls silent
in the absence of users.

Don't ask the charioteer
to yoke the thick-legged donkey,
        used to the crooked plow,
to your chariot strung with bells.

And for our lovely girl's sake,
her eyes cool as rain,
stay tonight
and go on tomorrow,
        man from the great waters.

In that shining big sea,
fishermen with big boats
        careless of the killer shark
dive for the right-spiralled oyster,

sound loud
the conch shells
that contain voices,

are met and welcomed
by bustling Koṟkai city
as they disembark on the long sandy coasts.

There,
you'll see
our good little town.

Centaṉ Kaṇṇaṉār
Akanāṉūṟu 350

What She Said
to her girl friend

Yesterday,
some people of this town
said about me,
she is the woman
of that man from the seashore

where great waves break
on the white sands.

Mother heard it
and asked me,
"Is that true?"
I said, under my breath,
"I'm burning."

Ammūvaṉār
Aiṅkuṟunūṟu 113

Four on the Tigerclaw Tree

What She Said

Friend, listen.
I'll not think any more
of that man on whose sandy shore

    birds occupy the tigerclaw tree
    and play havoc
    with the low flowering branches,

and my eyes will get some sleep.

What Her Girl Friend Said
to him

Her soft plump shoulders
that gave you pleasure once
on the sands

    where seabirds made a din
    on the tigerclaw tree

are now angry.

What She Said

My body,
    young mango leaf,
is now lovesick yellow

for that man
of the seashore

    where the stork sleeps alone
    in the flowering groves
    of tigerclaw trees.

What Her Girl Friend Said
on her wedding day

Our man of the seashore

    where the waves reach
    and shake the big branches
    of the small-leaved tigerclaw tree

has cleared once for all
the pallor of our lovesick girl.

Ammūvaṉār
Aiṅkuṟunūṟu, 142–145

What Her Girl Friend Said,
the lover within earshot, behind a fence

On the new sand
where fishermen,
their big nets
ripped apart by an angry sea,
dry their great hauls of fish

in a humming neighborhood
of meat smells,

a laurel tree blossoms
all at once in bright clusters
fragrant as a festival,

but this unfair town
is noisy with gossip.

And what with an unfair Mother too
keeping strict watch over us,

will our love just perish here
in sallow patches,

this love for our man
of the seashore

where petals
loosened by the traffic of birds
mix with the mud of the backwaters,

where the big-maned chariot horses galloping there
are washed clean
by the waves of the sea?

Ulōccaṉār
Naṟṟiṇai 63

What Her Girl Friend Said

to him, trying to dissuade him from his long journey

As they carry the white paddy of their land
to barter it for the salt of another,
crossing the long roads in carts
through sands white as moonlight,
taking whole families
who hate to be left behind,

the exodus of the salt merchants
leaves a city empty.

Seashore man,
you must be dense indeed:

what with the nasty cold wind
blowing through everything
and the misery of evenings
in your absence,

she is a water lily
in a dry bed
trampled by white herons
overfed on a whole shoal of fish.

She'll not last a day, believe me,
and you don't even think of it.

Anon.
Naṟṟiṇai 183

Six Said by the Concubines to Him

(1)

O yes, we've seen
your girl friend,
haven't we?

Splashing in the sea waves,
wetting even that wreath of water-thorn
in her hair?

(2)

O yes, we've seen
your girl friend,
haven't we?

Her gold ornaments fall
in the sand,
and all she does is ask

the small white snipe!

(3)

O yes, we've seen
your girl friend,
haven't we?

Making a din with her gaggle
of flashing girls,
she splashes
in the big cold wave,
doesn't she?

(4)

O yes, we've seen
your girl friend,
haven't we?

When the sea plays
with her sand-dolls,
she throws sand

and shrieks

at the sea,
doesn't she?

(5)

O yes, we've seen
your girl friend,
haven't we?

Delicate ornaments and garlands
of white dead nettle
on her young breasts,

she jerks them away
in a sulk,

doesn't she?

(6)

O yes, we've seen
your girl friend,
haven't we?

She gives her bud of a breast
with no milk yet

to a doll with a mouth
that cannot drink,

playing at giving suck,
doesn't she?

Ammūvaṉāṟ
Aiṅkuṟunūṟu 121–124, 127–128

What She Said

The fishermen who go
from the little town in the seaside groves
into the sea
wait in the thick shade of the blue laurel tree,
looking for the right time
to enter the cold wide waters,
spreading and drying meanwhile their nets
with many eyes and knots,

in the seaside of my man.

If only someone would go to him
and tell him,
"If Mother should ever hear
the scandal about us, it would be hard for me
to live here,"

maybe he'll take me then,

through those places where
the salt merchants trading in white rocksalt
wake up the cows sleeping on the long road
as they crunch their carts through the sand,
their loud wheels
scaring the black-legged white heron in the fields,

to his home town
surrounded by salt pans?

Ammūvaṉār
Naṟṟiṇai 4

What She Said

In his country of cool seas, they say,

on the screwpines with hanging roots
fat buds unfold
in leaves
like the wingfeathers
herons preen with their beaks,

and on the front yards
of his little seaside town
set in a grove,
the long waves come and go.

Though he has left
he is close to my heart,
living far away

in his country of cool seas.

Ceyti Vaḷḷuvaṉ Peruñcāttaṉ
Kuṟuntokai 228

What Her Girl Friend Said,
consoling her when she was distressed by the town's gossip

If it rains,
our town grows rich.
Ears of grain
cluster on the paddy grass
maned like horses.

When it's dry,
thorn bushes rise by the black waters,
the mud is parched.
But the dark shallows
yield a harvest of white salt.

Full of old ceremony,
this ancient town of ours
is always rich,
has kitchen smoke from frying fish
wafting through the streets
and on the beach
where tiny flowers dot the tigerclaw trees.

Yet, I must say, it has one fault.
The bees get high on the pollen
in the groves of black-branched laurel

and hum so loud

it's hard to hear the bells
of his tall chariot
when it comes.

Ulōccaṉār
Naṟṟiṇai 311

What She Said

When he said,
"I'll go! I'll go!"
I thought he was playing
at going, as usual,
and said,
"Go then,
leave me alone!"

Where is he now,
protective as a father,
O where?

The place between my breasts
is filled with tears,

a pool where
black-legged white heron
feed on fish.

Naṉṉākaiyār
Kuṟuntokai 325

PĀLAI: THE LOVERS' JOURNEY THROUGH THE WILDERNESS

What He Said
in the desert

In this long summer wilderness
seized and devoured by wildfire,

if I should shut my eyes
even a wink,

I see
dead of night, a tall house
in a cool yard, and the girl

with freckles
like kino flowers,

hair flowing as with honey,
her skin a young mango leaf.

Ōtalāntaiyār
Aiṅkuṟunūṟu 324

What Her Girl Friend Said
to her

Not happy with what he has,
piqued by the arrowy words
of cynics, he went.

But he'll come back.
Patience, my girl.

He went
into the woods
on the Ōṭai hills

where
like banners on a royal elephant
dry *ñemai* trees carry spiderwebs
that shiver in the wind,
and jungle elephants
grow faint and lean
in the heat,
mistake the webs for clouds,
lift long trunks painfully,
breaths bellowing in chorus
like trumpets for ritual dancers,

where
the tenacious wolf
drags at the carcass of the wild pig
he has killed,

and vultures drink the ooze of blood,
their red ears
like night lanterns that keep watch
in a field of wounded warriors.

Over such a mountain peak,
dipping into the valley of skies,
he went.

Pālaipāṭiya Peruṅkaṭuṅkō
("The Great Prince Who Sang *Pālai* Songs")
Akanāṉūṟu 111

What She Said,
thinking of him crossing the wilderness alone

The round blazing sun
creeps in the sky,
raging as a fire
in the forest,

and the silk-cotton tree
is leafless
yet in flower
without a bud,

like a long array
of red lamps
in the month of Kārttikai
lit happily
by bustling women,

in the fruitless forest
where the pools are dry, dusty.

If only
he'd spend the time with me,
it would go fast,

if only he'd walk swiftly with me
on the dunes
overhung with flowering boughs,
all fragrant,
where the forest stream flows now
and the sand
is laid out like a woman's bodice,

he could have what arms desire,
loving embraces,
body entering body,

and then my guiltless eyes
that now fill
ceaselessly like barren pools
fed by secret springs

could put aside
their daily sorrow
and find some sleep.

Auvaiyār
Akanāṉūṟu 11

What He Said

to his heart, arguing against further ambition and travel

A hen-eagle broods, sick
in the great branches
lifted to the sky,

in a neem tree
with cracked trunk and dotted shade

        where unschooled children
        scratch their squares
        on a rock
        flat as a touchstone
        and play marbles with gooseberries

        in that wilderness
        with fierce little settlements
        of marauders,
                the bow their only plow,

and as evening comes creeping in,
sapping my strength, what can I do
but think of her,

who is sweet as a deed
long wished for and done,

standing there
in this hour of memories
in front of a house lamp

blazing?

Iḷaṅkīraṉār
Naṟṟiṇai 3

What She Said
to her girl friend

No, we will not make vows to the ever-winning goddess
on the cracked, caverned ranges.
We will not tie sacred thread on our wrists.
We will not ask birds for omens.
We will not go looking for good signs.
No, we will not think a thought of him,

if he thinks he's strong enough
to stay wherever he has gone,
forgetting me

who cannot bear one blink of time
without him
who is the breath of my breath.

Koṟṟaṉ
Kuṟuntokai 218

Six on the Desert Ways

What He Said
in the wilderness

(1)

Even when I cross those places

where the hen-eagle,
parched head and chisel beak,
squawks on the dry forks
of spreading *ōmai* trees,

beyond the bare forest floors,
the several hills of alien languages,

her gentleness
goes with me.

(2)

They've come,
crossing even the hot forking desert paths

> where the sharp-toothed red dog of the jungle
> waits by the cactus clump
> to kill a wild pig
> for his mate
> now suffering pangs of labor,

all the way
they've come with you, O heart,

the gentle ways
of the woman you love.

(3)

In the desert

> where birds fear
> the summer rustle
> of pipal leaves
> and do not eat its fruit,
> and migrate elsewhere,

the narrow desert ways
do not trouble me:

I have for company
my love's gentleness.

(4)

The small-eyed elephant flinches,
afraid of burning
his big trunk,
        all streaked and spotted;
won't let it touch the ground.

The groves are charred
by the heat;
only bamboos stand tall
in these paths.

        Even in such a difficult stretch
        the thought
        of my girl's gentle ways

        keeps me cool.

(5)

A shower of small rain,
  and flowers appear all over:

but they're hot
  for the likes of me

who've left behind
  a sweet young love

to roam dried-up woods
  in wastelands.

(6)

Though we have come through
the hot dust of sunbeaten wastelands,

give up,
go no further:

her eyes fill,
her beauty is scattered,

as she thinks
of these, the sun's cruel burning places,

my girl
of glittering bangles

and delicate ornaments,

alone
in her heart's loneliness.

Ōtalāntaiyār
Aiṅkuṟunūṟu 321, 323, 325,
327, 328, 330

What He Said

The heart, knowing
no fear,
has left me
to go and hold my love
but my arms,
left behind,
cannot take hold.

So what's the use?

In the space between us,
murderous tigers
roar like dark ocean waves,
circling
in O how many woods
between us
and our arms' embrace?

Aḷḷūr Naṉmullai
Kuṟuntokai 237

What Her Girl Friend Said
before the elopement

The summer wind
blows through the wayside
sirissa trees,

the dry seedpods
rattle
like anklets with pebbles in them.

You can go with him now
through that desert,
my friend.

At last our man has given in.

Kuṭavāyiṟ Kīrattaṉār
Kuṟuntokai 369

What Her Mother Said

If a calving cow
chewed up her purslane creeper
growing near the house,

she'd throw the ball to the ground,
push away the doll,
and beat herself on her pretty tummy,
my little girl,
who knows now how to do things.

With a look tender as a doe's,
she'd refuse the milk
mixed with honey
her foster-mother and I would bring,
she'd sob and cry.

She was that way till yesterday.

Yet today,

trusting the lies
of a blackbeard man
she's gone
through the wilderness, laughing,
they say,
showing her white teeth
like new buds on a palm tree.

Anon.
Naṟṟiṇai 179

What the Passersby Said

to the lover eloping with the girl

The sun is down.
Listen
to that sound.

Don't go there
with your girl,
she's like a young she-elephant.

Forest bandits are at the fence,
long ringed lances
gripped as in the heat of battle,

signaling
with drum-taps, now,
and now again,

the coming of the traders.

Uṟaiyūr Mutukoṟṟaṉ
Kuṟuntokai 390

MULLAI: PATIENT WAITING AND HAPPINESS AFTER MARRIAGE

What She Said

Only the dim-witted say it's evening
when the sun goes down
and the sky reddens,
when misery deepens,
and the mullai *begins to bloom*
in the dusk.

But even when the tufted cock
calls in the long city
and the long night
breaks into dawn,
it is evening:
even noon
is evening,
to one who has no one.

Miḷaipperuṅ Kantaṉ
Kuṟuntokai 234

What She Said

Like milk
not drunk by the calf,
not held in a pail,

a good cow's sweet milk
spilled on the ground,

it's of no use to me,
unused by my man:

    my mound of love,
    my beauty
    dark as mango leaf,

    just waiting
    to be devoured
    by pallor.

Kollaṉ Aḻici (or Veḷḷi Vītiyār?)
Kuṟuntokai 27

What Her Girl Friend Said
to her

These fat cassia trees
are gullible:

the season of rains
that he spoke of
when he went through the stones
of the desert
is not yet here

though these trees
mistaking the untimely rains
have put out
long arrangements of flowers
on their twigs

as if for a proper monsoon.

Kōvatattaṉ
Kuṟuntokai 66

What She Said

Bird and beast
melancholy;
evening
a pitiless monotone.

As they shut the gates
through which men
of all kinds
enter,

the watchmen call out:

> Anyone else,
> anyone else
> to come?

Friend, only my lover
will not come.

Naṉṉākaiyār
Kuṟuntokai 118

What the Servants Said

to him, as he returned home

In encampments,

powerful elephants have fought the war,
the thunder of drums
resounds on the battleground,
the king has raised his victory banners.

Herds of cows and calves
come leaping into the forest
as herdsmen raise flutes
to their lips.

Your henchmen go rushing ahead,
the charioteer reins hard
to keep on the path
the fast-paced steeds with flying manes,

and when you return, my lord,

    wounds praised by poets,
    garlands on your chest,
    wearing cool fragrant sandal,
    smooth powders,

and enter
your house in triumphant joy,

where will it go, where
will it find a place,
                    that pallor
on the brow of our lady,
with eyes, lined with kohl,
darker than blue-dark flowers?

Maturaittamiḻkkūttaṉ Kaṭuvaṉ Maḷḷaṉār
Akanāṉūṟu 354

What She Said

Are there others too
with held-back tears
breaking out
from eyes streaked with red,
sick for love, lonely, confused,

who hear,

through the big rain
blown about by the wind
at midnight in the cold month

when the oxen
shake off the buzzing flies
again and again,

the poor thin chime
of clappers
in the crooked cowbells?

Veṇkoṟṟaṉ
Kuṟuntokai 86

What She Said

In the tiny village
on the hillside
where rainclouds play,

the grazing milch cows
remember their young
and return.

In the forest,
the white flowers
of the green-leaved jasmine
redden with the red evening,

and, friend,
I cannot bear it.

Vayilaṉṟēvaṉ
Kuṟuntokai 108

What He Said

Her arms have the beauty
of a gently moving bamboo.
Her large eyes are full of peace.
She is faraway,
her place not easy to reach.

My heart is frantic
with haste,

    a plowman with a single plow
    on land all wet
    and ready for seed.

Ōrēruḻavaṉār
("The Poet of the Plowman
  with the Single Plow")
Kuṟuntokai 131

What He Said
to his charioteer, on his way back

Rains in season,
forests grow beautiful.
Black pregnant clouds
bring the monsoons, and stay.
Between flower and blue-gem
flower on the bilberry tree
the red-backed moths multiply,
and fallen jasmines
cover the ground.
                                        It looks like
a skilled man's work of art,
this jasmine country.

Friend, drive softly here.
Put aside the whip for now.
Slow down
these leaping pairs of legs,
these majestic horses
galloping in style
as if to music.

Think of the stag, his twisted antlers

        like banana stems
        after the clustering bud
        and the one big blossom
        have dropped,

think of the lovely bamboo-legged doe
ready in desire:

if they hear the clatter
of horse and chariot,

how can they mate
at their usual dead of night?

Cīttalai Cāttaṉār
Akanāṉūṟu 134

Nine on Happy Reunion

What He Said

(1)

In this time of rain and thunder,

tormented without end,
heartsick
and sicker by the hour,
I've come hurrying,

dear girl,
to bring you back your beauty.

(2)

Because peacocks moved like you
and jasmine opened
like your brow
and the does had scared looks like you,

my girl,

thinking of you, your lovely brow,
I've come
faster than the rains.

(3)

As wild oxen bellowed,
answering the thunder of the sky's oxen,

as deer and mother-doe
moved in fear with their young,

and the rains began,

I hurried, thinking of you,
        your forearms
        decked with bangles.

(4)

The red earth
strewn with many kinds of flowers,
the woods no longer lonely,
my forest paths grew sweet
as I came home:

heart melting
every time I thought
of dense black hair
being braided, made up with flowers,

my girl with teeth sharp as thorns.

(5)

As the deer begin to hide
in the bush,
and the millet clusters with ears of grain
and the mountains grieve
as the rains pound and hammer,
look,

O you with those big quiet eyes,

your faraway lover
is back,
old companion of your arms.

Your hair,
fit place for opening buds,
would like flowers now.

What Her Girl Friend Said

(6)

As the cassias blossom
in small chains,
long red anthills send forth winged ants,
the animals have no appetite,

the season of rains
is on,
my dear girl,
and your man
who was in love with battle
has remembered

and come home.

(7)

Your arms are beautiful again,
the slipping bracelets
stay in place,
and your long streaked eyes
are lit up again,

now that the king
with his high-tusked elephants
is finished with his task,

and your man
with hills on his land
has come back, speeding
on his tall chariot.

(8)

Saying to himself,

"The white wild jasmine is in flower,
the climbing jasmine is in bud,
the forest has taken on the beauty
of the rains,
and if my love sees it
she will grieve,"

our lover has come back,
not giving himself anymore
to tasks of war,

so that your troubled beauty
may revive.

(9)

Her eyes
   lined with kohl
once grown yellow as cassia

now have their old beauty
of purple lilies in mountain pools

now that you,
tiger of the long battle-fronts of victorious war,
have come back.

Pēyaṉār
Aiṅkuṟūṉūṟu 491–493,
   495–500

What Her Girl Friend Said
to her lover on his return

Melt all the butter
from all the cows of all the cowherds
in the woods of Naḷḷi who has strong chariots,

mix it
with the steaming rice
from the dense white paddy
  of Toṇṭi fields,

heap them
in seven bowls
and offer it all to that crow
  that cawed those good omens

bringing guests
and an end to the grief
  that has been wasting my girl's arms.

Even so,
the offering
would still be too little.

Kākkai Pāṭiṉiyār Nacceḷḷaiyār
("Nacceḷḷai Who Sang of the Crow")
Kuṟuntokai 210

Seven Said by the Foster-Mother

(1)

The way
they lay together

    like deer, mother-doe,
    and fawn,

with their boy
between them, was very sweet:

neither in this world
hugged by the wide blue sea
nor in the one above

is such a thing easy to get.

(2)

Embracing the young mother from behind
as she hugged her little son,
the way
her husband lay:

    it was like music
    from the strings
    of a minstrel,

a thing of quality.

(3)

His heart swells
as he looks at his love,
now his wife,
and at his little son
named for a famous father—

his smile toothless,
his feet unsteady,
as he rolls
his tiny chariots of war.

(4)

Like the red flame
in the bowl
of a bedstead lamp
she lights up his house,

his jasmine country
jeweled by small towns,
all sorts of flowers
raised by sounding rains,

and she, the mother of his little son.

(5)

Embracing this woman
        who wants him as he wants her,

senses tuned all along
to the aphrodisiac
skill of his minstrel's lute,

he enjoys his love:
this man of soft meadows,
        jasmine meadows.

(6)

Minstrels sing the jasmine songs
of evening,
and his woman,

        brow shining, jewelry flaming,
        wears jasmine in her hair:

he's happy,
this excellent man
with his little son
who clears all evil

by just being there.

(7)

Evening in the yard,
a short-legged bed,
his wife his companion,
joy, laughter,
son clambering on his chest:

    but his minstrel's lute
    is much too melancholy.

Pēyaṉār
Aiṅkuṟuṉūṟu 401–403, 405,
407, 409, 410

MARUTAM: THE LOVER'S UNFAITHFULNESS, AFTER MARRIAGE

What She Said

In his country,

spotted crabs
born in their mother's death
grow up with crocodiles
that devour their young.

Why is he here now?

And why does he
take those women,

a jangle of gold bangles
as they make love,

only to leave them?

Ōrampōkiyār
Aiṅkuṟunūṟu 24

What She Said

As the lovely new flower
of the small-leaved cow's thorn

covers the meadows
and gives birth
to thorns,

my lover who was kind
now does evil,

and I'm sick at heart.

Aḷḷūr Naṉmullai
Kuṟuntokai 202

What Her Girl Friend Asked
and what she replied regarding his return

"From the long fronds
of a deserted talipot tree
with clusters thick and hard
like an old date-palm's,

a male bird calls to its mate,
and the listening tiger
roars in echo

on those difficult roads
where hot winds blow—

        but then your lover who went there
        has returned,
        has hugged you sweetly ever since
        and you've lain together
        inseparably
        in one place,

        and yet
        why do you look like a ruin,
        why do you grieve, my girl?"

So you ask, friend.
It could look like that to someone
who doesn't know.
                                What's the use
of longing faithfully
for his strong chest

        that's now like the cold beaches
        of Toṇṭi city
        famous in the mouths of many?

When love is gone,
what's copulation worth?

Anon.
Naṟṟiṇai 174

Five on the Riverside Cane

What She Said

(1)

Bees, six tiny legs and wings all lovely,
lay eggs in the hundred-petal lotus,

but the cane, hollow-stemmed as the bamboo,
destroys them all

in the watering places
near his town:
                    still,

        as I think of him,
        my bright bangles slip
        from my wrists.

(2)

Hovering like the heron
in the sky over the white cane-blossom
waving tall among leaves of grass,

he goes after new women.
My simple heart
stands empty.

(3)

In the full river
that plays with the sands
play the women in bright leaf-skirts

and our man of the old cane town
plays partner in their love play:

he belongs to our town,
yet he does not.

(4)

Like the high fanning tufts on swift horses
grows the white blossom of the cane
in his country of cool rivers.

And his women,
O they know nothing of sleep
even in the cosy small houses
of that sleepy town.

(5)

Green creepers planted inside the house
twine themselves with the cane outside
in his country of rivers.

Embarrassed
by his careless cruel ways, we say,
"He's a good man,"

but my round soft arms
say, "Not so, he's not,"
and grow thin.

Ōrampōkiyār
Aiṅkuṟunūṟu 11, 13, 15, 17, 18, 20

What She Said

Though he lives in the same town
he won't come into my street
and if he comes into my street
he'll not come near and hold me close.

He walks by, unseeing,
as if past the cremation grounds
of strangers,
and so my love,
once unashamed and senseless,
has fallen far away
like an arrow shot from a bow.

Pālai Pāṭiya Peruṅkaṭuṅkō
Kuṟuntokai 231

Five on the Crabs

What She Said

(1)

In his place, mother,

mud-spattered spotted crabs
sneak into holes at the root
of the nightshade.

O what's the point
of his marrying me then
with sweet talk,
and saying
these other things now?

(2)

In his place, mother,

field-crabs cut into the pink
purslane creeper,

hung with green pods,
reared with care in the house yard.

O he roves,

and women grieve
over his chest
till ornaments come loose on their limbs.

(3)

In his fields
overspread with sweet-basil,

crabs leave their females to go eat
the soft stem of the bindweed:

O how

can he be like this, mother,
knowing neither me
nor those others?

What Her Girl Friend Said
to the foster-mother

(4)

If you think, mother,
she's tormented by that goddess
of sweet-water places,

why then

is she growing so thin
that her ornaments come loose,
her soft arms grow sallow?

It's all for that man
from the riverside

where the crabs' feet
make designs
on the cool wet sands.

(5)

In his fields, mother,

rain beats down,
sentinels watch.

Yet crabs cut down
the fresh white seedling.

She has lain long enough
on his chest,
her mound of love
is spotted:

why does your daughter
still grieve,

grow sallow?

Ōrampōkiyār
Aiṅkuṟunūṟu 22, 24, 25, 26, 28, 29

What She Said
about her unfaithful, estranged husband

He's not from some country
beyond the hills,
or from a town so far
you can't see the trees.

He lives so near
I can't help but see him:
yet he acts distant,
like some holy sect
close only to a god.

There was a time when I
was close to him.

Neṭumpalliyattaṉ
Kuṟuntokai 203

What the Concubine Said
when she heard the wife complain
about the concubine's wiles

In lily ponds, the plump colorful buds
are forced open by bumblebees
on his cool seashore.

I sit with him,
we are two bodies.

We lie together,
we are close
as fingers around a bow.

He goes home,
I too am left
with a single body.

Villakaviraliṉār
("The Poet of the Fingers
Around a Bow")

Kuṟuntokai 370

What She Said

to him, after meeting his concubine

His palms spotless
as the petal
at the pollen center
of lotuses
that grow in old waters
where otters play,

his mouth lovely as coral,
making sweet baby talk
not yet uttered by tongue,
he makes everyone laugh.

Enchanting everyone,
he was playing alone in the street
with his toy chariot,
our son wearing gold ornaments—

when that woman of yours,
        burdened with gold,
        teeth sharp and lovely,
seeing your likeness in him,
thinking there was no one watching,
bent down happily
and called out to him,
"Come here, my love!"
and clasped him to her young breasts
borne down with necklaces.

Seeing her,
I couldn't move
but when she turned to me,
I held her close and I said,

"You young innocent,
don't be shy.
You too are a mother to him."

Her face fell
as one confessing a theft;
she stood scratching the ground
with her toenails.

Looking at her state,
didn't I too love her then,
thinking

"She's like the powerful goddess in the sky,
goddess of chaste wives,
and fit to be mother to your son?"

Cākalācaṉār
Akanāṉūṟu 16

What Her Girl Friend Said
when he sent a flattering minstrel on his behalf

Dear man from the city
of portia trees and rice fields
where

the small barbus fish
slips sometimes
from the heron's beak
and dives into the water
but fears ever after
the white bud of the lotus,

since one of your minstrels
was a liar,
all your minstrels must seem liars
to the women you abandon.

Ōrampōkiyār
Kuṟuntokai 127

What Her Girl Friend Said,
seeing her friend suffer in silent dignity
over her husband's infidelity

Tan like young mango leaf,
she plays Mother now.

Unworn blossom
shut away
all by itself in a pretty jar,
her body wilts.

Her man is from the cold seashore
where

blue lilies
rise on cane stalks
above green lily pads
in the black backwaters
with shoals of fish,

and, when it floods,
the dark flowers look
like the eyes
of women dipping in a pond.

She's too ashamed
to talk to us
about his cruelty;
so she chatters
to gloss it over.

Kayamaṉār
Kuṟuntokai 9

What Her Girl Friend Said,
when the woman was about to take back her unfaithful husband

Once she was the reason for his festivals.
Now she plays Mother.

And he's from the place
of the portia tree:

plowmen bend
its flowering branches
to spray themselves
with its yellow pollen
clustered like beans.

She has made such a secret
of his cruelty,

he will soon return to her,
shamefaced, I'm sure.

Ōrampōkiyār
Kuṟuntokai 10

What He Said
after a quarrel, remembering his wedding night

Serving in endless bounty
white rice and meat
cooked to a turn,
        drenched in ghee,
to honored guests,

and when the bird omens were right,
at the perfect junction
of the Wagon Stars with the moon
        shining in a wide soft-lit sky,

wedding site decorated, gods honored,
kettledrum and marriage drum
sounding loud the wedding beat,

the women who'd given her a bridal bath
—piercing eyes looking on, unwinking—
suddenly gone,

                her near kin
strung a white thread on her
with the split soft-backed leaves
of the sirissa,
and with the *aruku* grass,

        its sacred root a figurine,
        its buds cool, fragrant,
        dark-petalled, blue
        as washed sapphire,

        brought forth by the thundering skies
        of first rains in valleys
        where adolescent calves
        feed on them,

they brought her to me
decked in new clothes,
rousing my desire
even in the wedding canopy,
        wedding noises noisy as pounding rain,

on that first night,

and when they wiped her sweat,
and gave her to me,
        she splendid with ornament,
I said to her

        who was body now to my breath,
        chaste without harshness,
        wrapped all over in a robe
        new, uncrushed,

"It's hot. Sweat is breaking out
on that crescent, your brow.
Open your robe a little,
let the wind cool it,"

and even as I spoke,
my heart hasty with desire,
I pulled it off

and she stood exposed,
her form shining
like a sword unsheathed,
not knowing how to hide herself,

cried *Woy!*
in shame, then bowed, begged of me,
as she loosened her hair
undoing the thick colorful wreath
of broken lily petals

and, with the darkness of black full tresses,
hand-picked flowers on them
still luring the bees,

hid
her private
parts.

Viṟṟūṟṟu Mūteyiṉaṉār
Akanāṉūṟu 136

BOOK TWO

Puṟam Poems

Kings at War
Poets and Dancers
Chieftains
Lessons
War and After

The selections in this section are from two anthologies:

Puṟanāṉūṟu

Patiṟṟuppattu

KINGS AT WAR

Your bards are wearing lotuses
of gold

and the poets
are getting ready to ride
fancy chariots
drawn by elephants
with florid brow-shields:

is this right,
O lord rich in victories,

this ruthless taking
of other men's lands

while being very sweet to protégés?

Neṭṭimaiyār: on King
Peruvaḻuti
Puṟanāṉūṟu 12

Harvest of War

Great king,

you shield your men from ruin,
so your victories, your greatness
are bywords.

Loose chariot wheels
lie about the battleground
with the long white tusks
of bull-elephants.

Flocks of male eagles
eat carrion
with their mates.

Headless bodies
dance about
before they fall
to the ground.

Blood glows,
like the sky before nightfall,
in the red center
of the battlefield.

Demons dance there.

And your kingdom
is an unfailing harvest
of victorious wars.

Kāppiyāṟṟukkāppiyaṉār: on
Kaḷaṅkāykkaṇṇi Nārmuṭiccēral
Patiṟṟuppattu 35

Battle Scene

You might ask,

  "This Poṟai, so fierce in war,
  how big
  are his armies, really?"

Listen,
new travelers on the road!

As the enemy mob scampers and flees
and kings die on the field,

I've no body count
of those who kill as they fall,
and falling,
dance the victory dance
with lifted hands.

I've no count of the well-made chariots
that run all over them,
wheel-rims hardly worn,

nor of the horses, the men,
numberless,
I've not counted them.

And those elephants of his,
they cannot be pegged down,
they twist goads out of shape,

they stamp even on the moving shadows
of circling eagles,
and stampede like the cattle
of the Koṅkars
with pickax troops
on a wasteland of pebbles,

they really move, those elephants in his army:

I see them but I cannot count them.

Aricil Kiḻār: on Takaṭūr Eṟinta Peruñcēral Irumpoṟai
Patiṟṟuppattu 77

A Parade

Like a long line of high-flying herons
roused and disturbed
by the raincloud,

your armies move

murderous bull-elephants,
rows of shields,
splendor
of white flags waving
on chariots,

and the parade
is a great pleasure
to onlookers.

But as it overruns
and destroys enemy lands
to bring back a booty of ornaments,

it spells evil
to men in the camps
of those kings

who cross you
and clash
with your rage.

Peruṅkuṉṟūr Kiḻār: on
Kuṭakkō Iḷañcēral Irumpoṟai
Patiṟṟuppattu 83

A Woman in Love with a Captive King

My lord has great shoulders
though he now eats rice-pap in prison.

And I, outside his prison,
grow sallow as gold
for want of him.

When he enters the battlefield
and takes on those warriors
who brag at the festivals
in the great resounding city,

he is the swell and ebb of the sea
in the harbor

that terrifies sellers of salt.

Nakkaṇṇaiyār: on
Pōrvaikkōpperuṉar Kiḷḷi
Puṟanaṉūṟu 84

A King's Last Words,
in jail, before he takes his life

If a child of my clan should die,
if it is born dead,
a mere gob of flesh
not yet human,

they will put it to the sword,
to give the thing
a warrior's death.

Will such kings
bring a son into this world
to be kept now
like a dog at the end of a chain,

who must beg,
because of a fire in the belly,
for a drop of water,

and lap up a beggar's drink
brought by jailers,
friends who are not friends?

Cēramāṉ Kaṇaikkāl Irumpoṟai
Puṟanāṉūṟu 74

A Poet's Counsel
to warring clansmen

Your enemy is not the kind who wears
the white leaf of the tall palmyra

nor the kind who wears garlands
from the black-branched neem trees.

Your chaplets are made of laburnum,
your enemies are made of laburnum too.

When one of you loses
the family loses,

and it is not possible
for both to win.

Your ways show no sense of family:
they will serve only to thrill
alien kings

whose chariots are bannered,
like your own.

Kōvūr Kiḻār: to Neṭuṅkiḷḷi and
Nalaṅkiḷḷi
Puṟanāṉūṟu 45

A Poet's Counsel

to a cruel king when he was about to have his enemy's children trampled to death by elephants in a public place

You come from the line of a Cōḻa king
who gave his flesh
for a pigeon in danger,
        and for others besides,

and these children also come
from a line of kings
who in their cool shade
share all they have

lest poets,
those tillers of nothing
but wisdom,
should suffer hardships.

        Look at these children,
        the crowns of their heads are still soft.

        As they watch the elephants,
        they even forget to cry,

        stare dumbstruck at the crowd
        in some new terror
        of things unknown.

Now that you've heard me out,
do what you will.

Kōvūr Kiḻār: to Kiḷḷi Vaḷavaṉ
Puṟanāṉūṟu 46

King Kiḷḷi in Combat

With the festival hour close at hand,
his woman in labor,
a sun setting behind pouring rains,

the needle in the cobbler's hand
is in a frenzy
stitching thongs for a cot:

swifter, far swifter,
were the tackles of our lord
wearing garlands of laburnum,

as he wrestled with the enemy
come all the way
to take the land.

Cāttantaiyār: on
Pōrvaikkōpperuṉar Kiḷḷi
Puṟanāṉūṟu 82

POETS AND DANCERS

Pāri! Pāri! they cry,
these poets
with their good red tongues,
praising one man
in many ways:

yet it's not only Pāri,

the rains too
keep the world
going
in these parts.

Kapilar: on Pāri
Puṟanāṉūṟu 107

A Guide to Patrons:
one bard to another

Dear singer:

here you are,
a lute in your hand
that knows its grammar,
a hunger in your belly
that no one heeds,
clutching at your waist
a cloth of patches
with strange threads,
damp with sweat,
on a body aimless as a ruined man's,
and your large family
dulled by poverty.

You round the whole earth
and you're here
to ask
in a small voice
for help.
So listen.

In bannered camps,
his army slaughters
the murderous elephants of enemy kings,
leaves them wounded in pools of blood,
makes a slaughterhouse of the battlefield.

He is at Uṟaiyūr,
city of tall towers;
he takes up spears only against enemies
and he moves right into the heart of their country.

He is Kiḷḷi Vaḷavaṉ,

    he wears perfect garlands,
    his ornaments are flames
    of yellow gold.

Go to him,

and you don't even have to stand
at his great door.

Go, fill your eyes
with the chariots he gives away
in broad daylight.

Once you've seen him
you'll wear lotuses of gold, flowers
    no bee will touch,

and you don't even have to stand
there, at that door.

Ālattūr Kiḻār: on Kiḷḷi Vaḷavaṉ
Puṟanāṉūṟu 69

A Poet to a Dancer

Dancer!

A one-headed drum
hangs on one side of you,
a hollow drum
on the other;

your rice-bowl is turned
face down, waiting
for someone to turn it over
and fill it;

you wait on the edge
of this desert,
and you've few bangles
on your wrist.

If you wish to go,
he is not far
from here:

Añci, man of many spears,
is at battle,
and as he sets fire
to enemy camps,
black battle-smoke
swirls around his young elephants
like mists
around mountain peaks.

Go,

and forever your bowl
will glisten
with meat
larded and melting
like cakes of softest tallow.

He has the strength
to protect and care
though the times are troubled.

Bless him,
his works.

Auvaiyār: on Añci
Puṟanāṉūṟu 103

A King's Double Nature:
a guide to singers

His armies love massacre,
he loves war,
yet gifts
flow from him ceaselessly.

Come, dear singers,
let's go and see him in Naravu

where, on trees
no ax can fell,
fruits ripen, unharmed
by swarms of bees,
egg-shaped, ready
for the weary traveler
in fields of steady, unfailing harvests;

where warriors with bows
that never tire of arrows
shiver
but stand austere
in the sea winds
mixed with the lit cloud
and the spray of seafoam.

There he is,
in the town of Naravu,
tender among tender women.

Kākkaipāṭiṉiyār Nacceḷḷaiyār
("Nacceḷḷai Who Sang of the Crow")
Patiṟṟuppattu 60

The Price of Giving Too Much

Bless you, bless you,
Naḷḷi.

Now our minstrels
play morning pastorals
in the still drone of evening,

and in the morning
they play
on their lutes

evening's seaside songs:

> all because you, in your bounty,
> have taken on this business
> of giving and caring,
>
> our men
> have forgotten
> our traditions.

Vaṉparaṇar: on Naḷḷi
Puṟanāṉūṟu 149

The True Protocol of Poets

Protégés will come
toward a giver
from all four directions.

It's hard to know
the true protocol
of poets,
but it's easy to give.

Consider this well,
chieftain, generous giver,

and put aside
indiscriminate views

regarding poets.

Kapilar: on Malaiyamāṉ
Tirumuṭikkāri
Puṟanāṉūṟu 121

A Bard's Family

My mother grumbles,

> "I've lived too many days and years.
> Still my life isn't coming to an end."

She creeps about, taking little steps,
with a stick for a leg.
Her head of hair a scatter of threads,
eyes dim,
she is too old even to walk to the yard.

And my wife, her body gone sallow, is troubled
by pain and sickness;
breasts fallen,
squeezed and devoured by the many children
all about her;
needy, she picks the greens
in the garbage dump
hardly sprouting
in the very spot she had plucked before,
boils them in water
without any salt,
eats them without any buttermilk.
She has forgotten the look of well-cooked food.
Wearing unwashed tatters,
my wife who loves me
goes hungry,
blames the order of things.

You can make their hearts happy:
I know you are known for giving
like a raincloud

> that pours with thunder and lightning
> on wide fields

scorched and plowed by hunters
where millet, sown with rice,
is unable to ripen to rich dark grain,
arrested by the heat.

You can make my whole hungry family happy.

Yet, I'll take nothing,
not even a killer elephant with high tusks,
if it is not given happily.
But if you are pleased, and give
to please,
I'll even take a crab's-eye.

So, Kumaṇaṉ of the sharp spear,
lord born in a clan without a stain,
famed for its victories,
show me your grace
I ask you,
as I sing your praise.

Peruñcittiraṉār: on Kumaṇaṉ
Puṟanāṉūṟu 159

CHIEFTAINS

A Chariot Wheel

Enemies,
take care
when you enter
the field of battle
and face
our warrior

who is like a chariot wheel
made thoughtfully over a month
by a carpenter
who tosses off eight chariots
in a day.

Auvaiyār: on Atiyamāṉ
Neṭumāṉ Añci
Puṟanāṉūṟu 87

His Welcome

He welcomes us still
as on the first of days,

though we go there
not just one day,
or two days,
but many days
with many friends,

does Atiyamāṉ Añci
of the jeweled elephant
and the artful chariot.

Whether the time for gifts
comes right now
or is put off for later,

it's like fodder
left in reserve
on the elephant's tusk,

always there
at hand, waiting;
it won't become a lie.

O wishful heart,
do not scramble for it.

Bless him,
his works.

Auvaiyār: on Añci
Puṟanāṉūṟu 101

The Tiger

Forbearance of kinsmen's wrongs,
a good man's shame over other men's poverty,
honor without blemish in acts of war,
courtesy in the courts of kings:

these do not fit your chieftains,
they describe only our man.

His spear deadly,
his chest widened by the full, taut drawing
of bows,
our chieftain of the mountain tribes
wears a wreath of red glory lilies
on his head.

At sunset,
where the mountain heights
waylay the rain cloud,
herds of deer are uncertain
of their directions
in the green dusk,
the stag calls to his young mate
through the forest,

and the tiger waits
in his lair,
pricks up and leans his tan-colored ear,

listening.

Kuṟamakaḷ Iḷaveyiṉi: on
Ēraikkōṉ
Puṟanāṉūṟu 157

A Young Chieftain

The young bull
does not feel the yoke,
though the cart is loaded
with salt and things.

But who can
foresee the damages
when it dips into creeks
and climbs the hills?

So the salt merchants keep
a second safety axle
under the axletree.

You are such,

lofty one
with bright umbrellas of fame:

whoever lives in your shade,
living as under the fullest moon,

has any fear
of night?

Auvaiyār: on Pokuttel̲in̲i
Pur̲anān̲ūr̲u 102

A Cycle of Poems on Pāri and His Hill

His Hill

Pāri's Paṟampu hill
is quite a place.

Even if all three of you kings
should surround it
with your great drums of war,
remember
it has four things
not grown under the plows
of plowmen:

one, wild rice
grows in the tiny-leaved bamboos;
two, ripening jackfruit,
crammed with segments
of sweet flesh;
three, down below
grow sweet potatoes
under fat creepers;
four,
beehives break
as their colors ripen
to a purple,
and the rich tall hill
drips with honey.

The hill is wide as the sky,
the pools flash like stars.
Even if you have
elephants

ied to every tree there,
and chariots
standing in every field,
you will never take the hill.
He will not give in
to the sword.

But I know a way
to take it:

pick carefully
your lute-strings, string little lutes,
and with your dancing women
with dense fragrant hair
behind you,

go singing and dancing
to Pāri,

and he'll give you
both hill and country.

Kapilar: on Pāri
Puṟanāṉūṟu 109

Pāri's Hill Is Partial to Dancers

The great black hill
is a strange place indeed:

inaccessible to kings
who fight with spears,

yet open to any girl
with a drum in her hand,

her eyes lined with kohl
blueblack as the water lily,

if she should come
singing.

Kapilar: on Pāri
Puṟanāṉūṟu 111

That Month

That month
in that white moonlight,

    we had our father,
    and no one
    could take the hill.

This month
in this white moonlight,

    kings with drums
    drumming victory
    have taken over the hill,

and we
have no father.

Pāri's daughters: on the death
of Pāri
Puṟanāṉūṟu 112

Farewell to Pāri's Hill

With your wine jars open,
rams slaughtered,
endless dishes of meat, mince, rice,
your riches primed
to give according to each receiver's wish,

you made friends with us once.

Now Pāri is dead,
our hearts are muddy, our eyes are streaming;
we'll pray and bless
and take your leave,

Paṟampu, hill of fame,

    and we'll go our ways
    in search of men
    who are fit to touch
    the dark fragrant hair
    of Pāri's daughters,
    with many small bangles
    on their wrists.

Kapilar: to Pāri's Paṟampu hill
Puṟanāṉūṟu 113

A Memory of the Hill

Stand here, you can see the hill;
go far away, you still see it.

Like a scatter of fiber
after an elephant's meal
was the refuse
of the wine-press there,

the flowing wine
muddying the yards
in the hill
of our great chieftain,
giver of chariots.

Kapilar: on Pāri's Paṟampu hill
Puṟanāṉūṟu 114

Waterfalls and Liquor

Waterfalls sounded
on one side,

and on another,

the clear liquor
spilling over
when poured into the bowls
of minstrels

would turn the stones in its stream
as it flowed,

    on the hill
    of that sweet man
    bitter only to enemy kings
    with elephants
    and many spears.

But no more.

Kapilar: on Pāri
Puṟanāṉūṟu 115

Pāri's Green Land, Remembered

Even when black Saturn
smouldered in the sky,
even when comets smoked
and the silver star
ran to the south,

his crops would still come to harvest,
the bushes would flower,
large-eyed rows of wild cows
would calve in the yard
and crop the grass.

Because his scepter was just,

> the green land knew
> no lack of rains,
> there were many noble men,
> green-leaved jasmine
> flowered
> like the thorn teeth
> of young wildcats

in the country of Pāri,
father of those artfully bangled daughters.

Kapilar: on Pāri
Puṟanāṉūṟu 117

Then and Now

The clear pond,
once banked with boulders and round stones,
curved like the eighth-day moon,
now lies broken:

> so does cool Paṟampu,
> once the land
>
> of Pāri
>
> whose arms were strong, whose spears were sharp,
> whose chariots gleamed.

Kapilar: on Pāri's Paṟampu
Puṟanāṉūṟu 118

Others

Āy: A Gift of Elephants

Since those bards,

with their sweet songs
and small lutes
black-stemmed as whortleberries,

sang here and left,

the tall elephant-posts stand bare
without elephants.
Only wild peacocks
stay there with their kind.

They say,
the women here are left
only with wedding-chains
they can't give away,
and Āy's palace
is dim.

Yet
the houses of kings
with drums and riches,
fine foods spiced and sautéed
to fill only their own bellies,

they are unspeakable,
they are not a patch
on Āy's
empty palace.

Muṭamōciyār: on Āy Aṇṭiraṉ
Puṟanāṉūṟu 127

Āy: His Hill

When the ape
on the bough
of the jackfruit tree
in the town's commons

mistakes for fruit
the eye
on the thonged drumheads
hung up there by mendicant bards,

he taps on it,

and the sound rouses
the male swans below
to answering song

in Potiyil, that hill where the clouds crawl,
hill of Āy
with war anklets on his feet,

hill inaccessible
to great kings,

yet open to the approaches
of dancers.

Muṭamōciyār: on Āy
Puṟanāṉūṟu 128

Kāri Sober

If a man's drunk from morning on
and delighted with the crowd
in the court,
it's easy for him
to give away a chariot or two.

But the tall gold-covered chariots
given by Malaiyaṉ
of everlasting fame,

given when he's sober,

outnumber the raindrops
on the rich peaks of Muḷḷūr.

Kapilar: on Malaiyamāṉ
Tirumuṭikkari
Puṟanāṉūṟu 123

LESSONS

The Great Wagon

If the driver is good,
the great wagon

that's driven through the world
only under escort,
its wheels fitted well
to its body,

will give him
a smooth untroubled road.

If the man doesn't know
how to steer it,
it'll get stuck all day
in the mire, its enemy,
and trouble him
over and over again.

Toṇṭaimāṉ Iḷantiraiyaṉ
Puṟanāṉūṟu 185

This World Lives Because

This world lives
because

some men
do not eat alone,
not even when they get
the sweet ambrosia of the gods;

they've no anger in them,
they fear evils other men fear
but never sleep over them;

give their lives for honor,
will not touch a gift of whole worlds
if tainted;

there's no faintness in their hearts
and they do not strive
for themselves.

Because such men are,
this world is.

Iḷam Peruvaḻuti
Puṟanāṉūṟu 182

Not Rice, Not Water

Not rice,
not water,
only the king
is the life-breath
of a kingdom.

And it is the duty
of a king
with his army of spears
to know
he's the life
of the wide, blossoming kingdom.

Mōcikīraṉār (or
Mātimātirattaṉār)
Puṟanāṉūṟu 186

Earth's Bounty

Bless you, earth:

field,
forest,
valley,
or hill,

you are only
as good
as the good young men
in each place.

Auvaiyār
Puṟanāṉūṟu 187

Children

Even when a man has earned much
of whatever can be earned,
shared it with many,
even when he is master of great estates,

if he does not have
children

        who patter on their little feet,
        stretch tiny hands,
        scatter, touch,
        grub with mouths
        and grab with fingers,
        smear rice and ghee
        all over their bodies,
        and overcome reason with love,

all his days
have come to nothing.

Pāṇṭiyaṉ Aṟivuṭai Nampi
Puṟanāṉūṟu 188

Why My Hair Is Not Gray

If you ask me how it is
that I'm so full of years
and yet my hair is not gray,

it's because
my wife is virtuous,
my children are mature;

younger men wish
what I wish,
and the king only protects,
doesn't do what shouldn't be done.

Moreover, my town
has several noble men,
wise and self-possessed.

Picirāntaiyār
Puṟanāṉūṟu 191

Every Town a Home Town

Every town our home town,
every man a kinsman.

Good and evil do not come
from others.
Pain and relief of pain
come of themselves.
Dying is nothing new.
We do not rejoice
that life is sweet
nor in anger
call it bitter.

Our lives, however dear,
follow their own course,

rafts drifting
in the rapids of a great river
sounding and dashing over the rocks
after a downpour
from skies slashed by lightnings—

we know this
from the vision
of men who see.

So,
we are not amazed by the great,
and we do not scorn the little.

Kaṇiyaṉ Pūṅkuṉṟaṉ
Puṟanāṉūṟu 192

Relations

Like a hunted deer
on the wide white
salt land,

a flayed hide
turned inside out,

one may run,
escape.

But living
among relations
binds the feet.

Ōrērul̲avan̲ār
("The Poet Of The Single
Plow")
Pur̲anān̲ūr̲u 193

WAR AND AFTER

A Young Warrior

O heart
sorrowing
for this lad

once scared of a stick
lifted in mock anger
when he refused
a drink of milk,
now
not content with killing
war elephants
with spotted trunks,

this son
of the strong man who fell yesterday

seems unaware of the arrow
in his wound,

his head of hair is plumed
like a horse's,

he has fallen
on his shield,

his beard still soft.

Poṉmuṭiyār
Puṟanāṉūṟu 310

Five Elegies

Elegy (1)

This bright burning pyre
of black half-burned faggots,
pieces picked as if by a gypsy
in a field fire,

may it burn brighter
till it burns down to a handful.
Or rise in flames
and reach out to heaven.

The fame of our sun-like king,
his white umbrellas cool
as the moon,

will not blacken,
will not die.

Auvaiyāṟ: on Añci
Puṟanāṉūṟu 231

Elegy (2)

Let day, let night, come no more.
Let all my days come to nothing.

We have put peacock feathers
on his headstone
and poured bark-wine
in little bowls for him:

will he accept them,
who didn't accept a whole country
of mountain peaks?

Auvaiyār: on Añci
Puṟanāṉūṟu 232

Elegy (3)

If he found a little liquor,
he would give it to us.

If he had more,
he would drink happily
while we sang.
Where is he now?

If he had even a little rice,
he shared it
in many plates.
Where is he now?

If he had more,
he shared it
in many more plates.
Where is he now?

He gave us
all the flesh
on the bones.
Where is he now?

Wherever spear and arrow flew,
he was there.
Where is he now?

With his palms scented
with lemon grass,
he caressed my hair
smelling of meat.
Where is he now?

The spear that pierced his chest
pierced at once
the wide eating bowls
of great and famous minstrels,

pierced many begging palms,

and, dimming the images in the eyes
of men he sheltered,
it went right through the subtle tongues
of poets
skilled in the search
for good words.

Where is he now,
father, mainstay,
king?

Where is he now?

No more,
no singers any more
nor anyone to give anything
to singers.

As in the cold waters
jalap flowers blossom,
large, full of honey,
but die untouched, unworn,

there are many now living
and dying,

without giving
one thing
to others.

Auvaiyār: on Añci
Puṟanāṉūṟu 235

Elegy (4)

He has held
women's arms
  covered with bangles;

has worn flowers
  plucked from young guardian trees;

covered himself with sandal,
  cool and fragrant;

killed off dynasties
  of enemies;

and praised friends.

He would not buckle
to the strong, nor swagger
  with the meek;

never knew how to beg a favor
  nor how to refuse one;

in the courts
his good name was a presence,
  visible.

He faced oncoming armies,
looked on the backs of fleeing ones,
galloped his horses faster than thought,
drove chariots in the long city streets,
  rode tall and extraordinary elephants.

He emptied for others
pitchers of sweet liquor,
  quelled the hunger of delighted minstrels.

He brought clarity, and put aside
   confusing words.

Thus he did
   all that needed doing.

      Now sever his head,
      or let it be.
      Bury him
      or burn him.
      It matters little.

Do what you will
with this man
   who loved a good name.

Pēreyin̲ Muruvalār: on Nampi
   Neṭuñcel̲iyan̲
Pur̲anān̲ūr̲u 239

Elegy (5)

The young will not wear it.
Bangled women will not pluck it.
Neither minstrel, nor his singing woman,
will bend this stalk of jasmine
with the crook of a lute
to wear it in their hair.

Cāttaṉ of the Big Lance
who mastered men
with his manhood,
is gone.

Why do you bloom now,
jasmine,
in this land of Ollai?

Kuṭavāyiṟ Kīrattaṉār: on
Peruñcāttaṉ
Puṟanāṉūṟu 242

Ascetics

A Charmer Turned Ascetic

We've seen him before
in a house
spaced as in a picture,

with small-bangled women,
mirror images
of the goddess on the hill:

this charmer,
how he made them all lovesick
till their ornaments came loose.

Now he bathes
among bamboos
in the tall hill's waterfalls,

lights red fires
with wood
that wild elephants bring,

and dries the twists of hair
that hang down his back.

Mārippittiyār (or Māṟpittiyār)
Puṟanāṉūṟu 251

A Hunter Once, Now an Ascetic

Bathing in the roaring white waterfall
has changed his color.
His matted locks are brown leaves
on a blinding tree,
and he is now plucking for food
a bunch of thick leaves
from a bindweed.

He was a hunter once.
He had a net
of words,
and he caught peacocks
that wandered innocently
into his yard.

Mārippittiyār
Puṟanāṉūṟu 252

Wives, Widows, and Horses

A Woman and Her Dying Warrior

I cannot cry out,
I'm afraid of tigers.
I cannot hold you,
your chest is too wide
for my lifting.

Death
has no codes
and has dealt you wrong,
may he
shiver as I do!

Hold my wrist
of bangles,
let's get to the shade
of that hill.
Just try and walk a little.

Vaṉparaṇar
Puṟanāṉūṟu 255

An Urn for Burial

Potter,
        O potter,

I've come with him
through narrow places

like a tiny white lizard
hugging the spoke
of a cart wheel.

Be kind,
make me an urn
for his burial
in the wide earth

and make it
wide enough
for me too,

        you who make pitchers
        for this city,
        this wide, old city.

Anon
Puṟanāṉūṟu 256

Widows' Rice

The little white lilies,
poor things,

gave me tender leaf
to wear, when I was young.

Now, my great husband is dead,
I eat at untimely evening hours

and the lilies give me lily seed,
a widow's rice.

Okkūr Mācāttaṉar
Puṟanāṉūṟu 248

The Horse Did Not Come Back

The horse did not come back,
his horse did not come back.
All the other horses have come back.

The horse
of our good man,

    who was father in our house
    to a little son
    with a tuft of hair
    like a plume on a steed,

it did not come back.

Has it fallen now,
his horse
that bore him through battle,

has it fallen
like the great tree
standing at the meeting place
of two rivers?

Erumai Veḷiyaṉār
Puṟanāṉūṟu 273

On Mothers

Mothers (1)

That dignified old woman,

with white hair
that has given up
all fragrant things,

and withered breasts
with nipples like eyes
crinkled as the ironwood seed,

she has a much-loved son who, all alone,

like a drop of curd
flicked by a childish milkmaid's
fingernail
curdling a whole pitcher of milk,

brought grief
to an army of enemies.

Maturaippūtaṉ Iḷanākaṉār
Puṟanāṉūṟu 276

Mothers (2)

The old woman's hair
was white, feather
of the fisher heron.

Her delight

when she heard
that her son fell in battle
felling an elephant,

was greater
than at his birth,

and her tears
were more than the scatter of drops
hanging from all the great swaying bamboos
after the rains
on the Bamboo Mountains.

Pūṅkaṇuttiraiyār
Puṟanāṉūṟu 277

Mothers (3)

The old woman's shoulders
were dry, unfleshed,
with outstanding veins;
her low belly
was like a lotus pad.

When people said
her son had taken fright,
had turned his back on battle
and died,

she raged
and shouted,

> "If he really broke down
> in the thick of battle,
> I'll slash these breasts
> that gave him suck,"

and went there,
sword in hand.

Turning over body after fallen body,
she rummaged through the blood-red field
till she found her son,
quartered, in pieces,

and she rejoiced
more than on the day
she gave him birth.

Kākkaipāṭiṉiyār Nacceḷḷaiyār
("Naceḷḷai Who Sang of the Crow")
Puṟanāṉūṟu 278

Mothers (4)

There, in the very middle
of battle-camps
        that heaved like the seas,

pointing at the enemy
        the tongues of lances,
new-forged and whetted,

urging soldiers forward
        with himself at the head
in a skirmish of arrow and spear,

cleaving through
        an oncoming wave of foes,
forcing a clearing,

he had fallen
in that space
        between armies,
his body hacked to pieces:

        when she saw him there
        in all his greatness,
        mother's milk flowed again
        in the withered breasts
        of this mother
        for her warrior son
        who had no thought of retreat.

Auvaiyār
Puṟanāṉūṟu 295

Mothers (5)

You stand against the pillar
of my hut and ask:
        Where is your son?

I don't really know.
This womb was once
a lair
for that tiger.

You can see him now
only on battlefields.

Kāvaṟpeṇṭu
Puṟanāṉūṟu 86

A Mother's List of Duties

To bring forth and rear a son is my duty.
To make him noble is the father's.
To make spears for him is the blacksmith's.
To show him good ways is the king's.

And to bear
a bright sword and do battle,
to butcher enemy elephants,
and come back:

that is the young man's duty.

Poṉmuṭiyār
Puṟanāṉūṟu 312

A Leaf in Love and War

The chaste trees, dark-clustered,
blend with the land
that knows no dryness;
the colors on the leaves
mob the eyes.

We've seen those leaves
on jeweled women,
on their mounds
of love.

Now the chaste wreath lies slashed
on the ground, so changed, so mixed
with blood, the vulture snatches it
with its beak,
thinking it raw meat.

We see this too
just because a young man
in love with war
wore it for glory.

Veṟipāṭiya Kāmakkaṇṇiyār
Pur̄anāṉūṟu 271

Peace Poem

Waist thin as the purslane creeper,
gait heavy as with grief,

the young brahman came at night
and entered the fortress quickly.

The words he spoke
were few,

and the ladders, the wooden bolts,
came down,

and the war bells
were loosened

from the flanks
of the veteran elephants.

Maturai Vēḷācāṉ
Puṟanāṉūṟu 305

When a King Asks for a Chieftain's Daughter

The king scrapes the sweat
off his brow
with the blade of his spear
and says terrible things.
The girl's father
rants as well
and will not speak softly.

This is their natural way of speaking.

And come to think of it,
this lovely girl,

> sharp teeth, cool eyes
> streaked with red,
> skin the color
> of young mango leaf,

this goddess,

like a fire
sparked by the wood itself,

will devastate
the very place of her birth.

Maturai Marutaṉ Iḷanākaṉār
Puṟanāṉūṟu 349

Where the Lilies Were in Flower

Fish leaping
in fields of cattle;

easy unplowed sowing
where the wild boar has rooted;

big-eyed buffalo herds
stopped by fences of lilies
flowering in sugarcane beds;

ancient cows bending their heads
over water flowers
scattered by the busy dancers
swaying with lifted hands;

queen's-flower trees full of bird cries,
the rustle of coconut trees,
canals from flowering pools
in countries
with cities sung in song:

> but your anger
> touched them, brought them terror,
> left their beauty in ruins,
> bodies consumed by Death.

The districts are empty, parched;
the waves of sugarcane blossom,
stalks of dry grass.
The thorny babul of the twisted fruit
neck to neck with the giant black babul.

The she-devil with the branching crest
roams
astraddle on her demon,
and the small persistent thorn

is spread in the moving dust
of ashen battlefields.

Not a sound, nothing animal,
not even dung,
in the ruins of public places
that kill the hearts of eager men,
chill all courage,
and shake those who remember.

But here,
the sages have sought your woods.
In your open spaces, the fighters play
with bright-jeweled women.
The traveler is safe on the highway.
Sellers of grain shelter their kin
who shelter, in turn, their kin.

The silver star will not go near
the place of the red planet: so it rains
on the thirsty fields.
Hunger has fled
and taken disease with her.

Great one,
your land blossoms
everywhere.

Kūmaṭṭūr Kaṇṇaṉār: on Imayavarampaṉ Neṭuñcēralātaṉ
Patiṟṟuppattu 13

In Praise of a Cremation Ground

The jungle spreads.
Cactuses grow.
Owls hoot even by day.
And haunted by she-demons
gaping in the light of crematory fires,
this ancient smouldering cremation ground
looks fearful.
Lovers' tears
wept from the heart
quench the burning white
ash and bones.

> This ground,
> it is the end
> of everyone in the world,
> looks upon the backs of all men,
> and hasn't seen anyone yet
> who will look upon *its* back.

Kataiyaṅ Kaṇṇaṉār
Puṟanāṉūṟu 356

A Poet's Memory Is Counsel

"When, in summer,
the fruit of the palm dries
and becomes stone,

when the fruit of the forest neem
shrivels,

when watering places crack their beds,
and unadapting fish, white as silver,
swim south and leave behind
a fish famine,

dear young warrior,

put me among those you remember
on such days,"

                    said my lord once,
and gave me gifts,
my lord of lasting glory.

He's now where no one can reach him.
Yet if one could go,
he's not the kind who'd be hard to see.

He, old king Ātinuṅkaṉ,
would catch the young
of jungle elephants
and make the soft-browed
mother beast grieve.
He'd tie them up in the public places
of his good city
which had a whole hill
in the middle of it.

Like him,

my lord of Vēṅkaṭam
where waterfalls
fall through rock,

you, Nallērmutiya,
who do not rise at once to run
wherever your heart goes,

you too must give
good things to hunger's households,
give
and give till misery ends.

May your women,
their mounds of love wide and soft,
may they never hear
in the long yards of your house

the funeral drums of grief.

Kaḷḷil Āttiraiyaṉār: to Nallēr
Mutiyaṉ
Puṟanāṉūṟu 389

BOOK THREE

Poems in a Different Key

What He Said

When love is ripe beyond bearing
and goes to seed,
men will ride even palmyra stems
as if they were horses;

will wear on their heads
the reeking cones of the erukkam bud
as if they were flowers;

will draw to themselves
the laughter of the streets;

and will do worse.

Pēreyiṉ Muruvalār
Kuṟuntokai 17

The selections in this section are from *Kalittokai*

What She Said

"O your hair," he said,
"it's like rainclouds
moving between
branches of lightning.
It parts five ways
between gold ornaments,
braided with a length of flowers
and the fragrant screwpine.

"O your smiles, your glistening teeth,
words sheer honey,
mouth red as coral,
O fair brow,
I want to tell you
something,
listen, stop and listen,"

he said, and stopped me.

Came close,
to look closer
at my brow, my hands, my eyes,
my walk, my speech,
and said, searching
for metaphors:

> "Amazed, it grows small, but it isn't the crescent.
> Unspotted, it isn't the moon.
> Like bamboo, yet it isn't on a hill.
> Lotuses, yet there's no pool.
> Walk mincing, yet no peacock.
> The words languish, yet you're not a parrot,"
>
> and so on.

On and on he praised my parts
with words gentle and sly,
looked for my weakening
like a man with a net
stalking an animal,

watched me
as my heart melted,
stared at me
like a butcher at his prey,

O he saluted me, saluted me,
touched me O he touched me,
a senseless lusting elephant
no goad could hold back.

Salute and touch,
and touch again he did,

but believe me, friend,
I still think he is not really

a fool by nature.

Kapilar
Kalittokai 55

What She Said
to her girl friend

O you, you wear flowers of gold,
their colors made in fire,
complete with pollen,
while the flowers on creeper and branch
are parched, waterless.
Your lovely forearm stacked
with jeweled bracelets,
shoulders soft as a bed of down,

is it right not to let me
live at your feet?
he said.

And didn't let go at that,
but stayed on to grab
all my hair
scented with lemon grass,
my hair-knot held together
by the gold shark's-mouth,
and with a finger
he twisted tight
the garland in my hair
and smelled it too.

Not only that, he took
my fingers
(unfolding now
like crocus buds,
I suppose)

to cover his bloodshot eyes
and fetched a huge sigh,
blowing hot like a blacksmith
into his bellows.

And,

like a deluded bull-elephant
fondling with his trunk
his beloved female,

he fondled my young painted breasts
till the paint rubbed off
on his rough hands.
Then he stroked me all over,
just about everywhere.

Yet friend,
with that act of his
I was rid
of all my troubles.

And I tell you this
only so that you can go
and persuade Mother:

May the sweet smells
of my marriage in our house
cling to no man
but him,
and that will be good.

It will guarantee a lasting place for us
in this world that doesn't last.

Kapilar
Kalittokai 54

What She Said

to her girl friend, and what her girl friend said in reply

"Friend,
like someone who gets drunk secretly
on hard liquor
till his body begins to ooze with it,
and goes on to brag shamelessly
till listeners shiver,
and then gets caught
with the stolen liquor in his hand,

I too got caught
with my secret in my hands:

my goatherd lover's
string of jasmine
that I'd twined in my hair
fell before my foster-mother
as she loosened my hair
to smear it with butter,

and embarrassed her
before Father, Mother,
and others in the house.

And she
didn't ask a thing about it,
or get angry,
but like someone
shaking off a live coal
she shook it off
and moved into the backyard.

Then I
dried my hair perfumed with sandal,
knotted it,
and picking up the end

of my blue flower-border dress
    that comes down to the floor
I tiptoed in fear
and hid
in the thick of the forest."

"O you got scared because of that?
No fears. Even as you wore
your young man's garlands,
they too have conspired
to give you to him.

They'll pour soft sand
in the wide yard,
put curtains all around,
and make a wedding there
very soon.
    Not only all day today,
but all night yesterday,
we've been scheming
to do just that."

Uruttiraṉ
Kalittokai 115

The Girl Friend Describes the Bull Fight

With the first rains

white clusters of the wild jasmine
backed by fresh thorn
are budding
on nodes once dry
in the cool rain lands.

The bud of the glory lily
looks like a ladle first,
then becomes a fire
when the red petals open
gathering the embers,
and it sways like a drunk.

The bilberry, flowering,
gives nothing but blue gems.

Weaving such blossom
in their wreaths,
cowherds vie with all they have,
enter the stalls
to let loose the bulls,
horns whittled sharp
as the Lord's own pickaxes.

There, in the middle ground,
where the brides wait,
men gather
again and again
ready to master the bulls,
sounding like rumbling and thunder,
raising dust clouds, and smoke,

offer the right things
to the gods
in watering places,
under the banyan tree
and the ancient mango.

There, they leap into the field.

Look, the bull,
raised horns and skin tawny
as certain silkmoths,
he skewers to death
the cowherd who sprang
heedless of the look in the animal's eyes,
carries the carcass high and shakes it
on his horns,

> like the warrior Bhīma
> making good his oath
> sworn among enemies,
> cleaving the heart
> of the man
> who dared put a hand
> to the tresses
> of his lovely wife.

Look at that black bull,
a moon-mark on his brow,
carry and shake the cowherd,
skewered and gutted
(the wreaths on his head
were flowers once on the caverned hills):

> like the raging androgynous god,
> whose one half is His woman,
> who dances at the end of time
>   when lives wear all their sorrows,
> cleaves the heart of the Death-god,

that rider of buffaloes,
and feeds Death's own guts
to His famished barbaric minions.

Look at that other bull
with spotted ears,
smooth reds
on his white body.
Teased by the fighters,
he throws that daredevil, that herdsman,
with the points of his horns,

like Aśvatthāma in grief and rage
not mindful of the darkness
whirling
on his shoulders
that eunuch
who slew his father.

But now the herdsmen
play flutes,
good omens
for you and your man
wearing blue-gem bilberry flowers.

[*Saying this, the girl friend went to the man and said:*]

That bull is wilder
than an elephant
gone wild:
do not loosen
your hand's grip
on him,
and the shoulders of our girl
will bring you victory flags.

Only to that man
who takes on that murderous bull,

carries a staff on his shoulder,
plays melancholy notes on his flute,
we will give our girl
with dark flowing hair.

Among men who take on a bull,
no one is equal to me, says he,
standing among the cows,
bragging of his power.

Surely, one day, not too far,
he will take us too:
for, looking at him,
my left eye throbs,
which is a good omen.

There, the bulls are faint,
and the men have wounds all over.
The cowherd girls
with dark fragrant hair,
taking hints
from their herdsman-lovers,
move into the cool groves
of jasmine.

Uruttiraṉ
Kalittokai 101

What She Said

to her girl friend, after a tryst at night
(which turned out to be a fiasco)

My well-dressed friend,
listen to what happened.
It has set the whole village laughing.

It's the dead of night, very dark,
no sign of life,
and I'm waiting
all dressed up, lovely shawl,
best jewels,
for our soft broad-chested man,

when that old cripple, that brahman
turns up,
the one you're always asking me to respect,
bald head, rough blanket,
hands and legs shortened by leprosy,
the fellow who never leaves our street.

He bends low
to take a good look at me
and says,
"Standing here
at this unearthly hour?
Who are you?"

He won't leave my side
like an old bull
who has sighted hay;
he opens his satchel, saying,
"Lady, come, have some betel, won't you?"

I stand there, say nothing.
"Listen, girl," he says,
stepping back a little.

"I've caught you.
I'm a demon too, but not your kind.
Be good to me. If you trouble me,
I'll grab all the offerings of this village,
and you'll get nothing."

And he jabbers on.
I can see by now the old fellow is a bit scared,
maybe thinking I'm some demon woman,
so I pick up a fistful of sand and throw it
in his face, and he howls and howls.

It was as if a trap laid by hunters
for a tiger, a fearless, striped, cruel-eyed tiger,
had caught instead a puny jackal.

What a sight for someone
waiting to see a lover!
The whole village is laughing
at this old brahman whose life
is a daily farce.

Kapilar
Kalittokai 65

The Hunchback and the Dwarf
A Dialogue

Hunchback woman,
the way you move is gentle
and crooked as a reflection
in the water,
                    what good deeds
did you do that I should want you so?

          O mother! (she swore to herself) Some
          auspicious moment made you dwarf,
          so tiny you're almost invisible,
          you whelp born to a man-faced owl,
          how dare you stop us to say
          you want us? Would such midgets
          ever get to touch such as us!

Lovely one,
                    curvaceous,
                                        convex
as the blade of a plough,
you strike me with a love
I cannot bear.
                    I can live
only by your grace.

          (Look at this creature!)
          You dwarf, standing piece of timber,
          you've yet to learn the right approach
          to girls. At high noon
          you come to hold
          our hand and ask us to your place.
          Have you had any women?

Good woman,
                    your waist is higher

than your head, your face a stork,
plucked and skinned,
with a dagger for a beak,
listen to me.
If I take you in the front, your hump
juts into my chest; if from the back
it'll tickle me in odd places.
So I'll not
even try it. But come close anyway and let's touch
side to side.

Chi, you're wicked. Get lost! You half-man!
As creepers hang on only to the crook of a tree
there are men who'd love to hold this hunch
of a body close, though nothing fits. Yet, you lecher,
you ask for us sideways. What's so wrong
with us, you ball, you bush of a man.
Is a gentle hunchback type far worse than a cake
of black beans?

But I've fallen for you
(he said, and went after her).
O look, my heart,
at the dallying of this hunchback!

Man, you stand
like a creepy turtle stood up by somebody,
hands flailing in your armpits.
We've told you we're not for you. Yet you hang around.
Look, he walks now like Kāma.

Yes, the love-god with arrows, brother to Cāma.
Look at this love-god!
Come now, let's find joy,
you in me, me in you; come, let's ask and tell
which parts we touch.

I swear by the feet of my king.

All right, O gentle-breasted one. I too will give up
mockery.
            But I don't want this crowd in the palace
laughing at us, screaming when we do it,
"Hey, hey! Look at them mounting,
leaping like demon on demon!"

                                    O shape
of unbeaten gold, let's get away from the palace
to the wild jasmine bush. Come,
let's touch close, hug hard,
and finish the unfinished:
then we'll be
like a gob of wax on a parchment
made out in a court full of wise men,
and stamped
to a seal.

            Let's go.

Maruta͟ṉiḷanākaṉār
Kalittokai 94

BOOK FOUR

Religious Poems

Red is the battlefield
as he crushes
the demons,

red his arrow shafts,

red the tusks
of his elephants:

this is the hill
of the Red One
with the whirling anklets,

the hill of red glory lilies,
flowers of blood.

Tipputtōḷār
Kuṟuntokāi 1

The selections in this section are
from two late classical anthologies:

Pattuppāṭṭu
Paripāṭal

Murukaṉ: His Places

Where goats are slaughtered,
where grains of fine rice are offered
   in several pots with flowers,
and His cock-banner is raised
in the festival of festivals
for many towns around;

wherever devotees praise
and move His heart;

where His spear-bearing shamans
set up yards
for their frenzy dance;

and in forests, parks,
lovely islets in rivers,
streams, pools, certain spots
   like four-way crossroads, meeting places,
cadamba oaks in first flower;

in assemblies under the main tree
and in town halls;

in sacred pillars;

and in the awesome vast temple
where the daughter of the hill tribe
worships

      raising a banner with His splendid bird on it,
      patting white mustard seed into ghee,
      chanting wordlessly her special chants,
      bowing
      and scattering flowers,
      wearing two cloths
         different in color and kind,

threads of crimson on her wrists,
scattering parched grain
and offering soft white rice
   mixed with the blood
   of strong fattened large-footed rams
in small offerings in several dishes,
sprinkling sandal fragrances
with yellow turmeric,
cutting together red oleander
   and big cool garlands
and letting them hang,

blessing the towns
   on the rich hill-slopes,
offering the sweet smoke of incense,
singing *kuṟiñci* songs
   while the roar of waterfalls
   mixes with the music of instruments,
spreading red flowers,
spreading fearful blood-smeared millet,

where the daughter of the hill tribe
sounds Murukaṉ's favorite instruments
and offers worship to Murukaṉ
till He arrives
and comes into her
to terrify enemies and deniers:

in that place then
they sing till the dancing yards echo,
they blow all the horns at once,
ring all the crooked bells,
bless His elephant
   with a peacock-shield on his forehead
who never runs from battle.

There
the suppliants offer worship,

ask and ask
as if to ask is to be given already.

He dwells in all such places
and I speak what I truly know.

Nakkīraṉār
Tirumurukāṟṟuppaṭai: 6
("A Guide to Lord Murukaṉ")

Tirumāl

In fire, you are the heat.
    In flowers, you are the scent.
Among stones, you are the diamond.

In words, you are truth.
    Among virtues, you are love.
In a warrior's wrath, you are the strength.

In the Vedas, you are the secret.
    Of the elements, you are the first.

In the scorching sun, you are the light.
    In the moonlight, you are the softness.

Everything, you are everything,
the sense, the substance, of everything.

Kaṭuvaṉ Iḷaveyiṉaṉār
Paripāṭal 3, lines 63–68

Hymn to Tirumāl (Viṣṇu)

1. *The Time of the Boar*

When the sun and the moon,
  given to alternations
  from the oldest times,
  went out,

  and the fresh golden world above
  and the earthen one below
  were ruined,

  there were ages of absence
  even of sky
  rolling time after time.

Sound was born first
  in the first age of sheer sky—
  womb of every growing germ
  though yet without forms,

then the ancient age of winds
  driving all things before them,

the age of mist and cool rain
  falling,

and when all four elements
  lay drowned in the old flood,
  the particles of earth
  lay there,

  recovering their own
  natures, getting themselves
  together;

then came the age of great earth
  lying potential
  in them all;

beyond the times counted
  in millions, billions, trillions,
  quadrillions, and zillions,

came the time of the Boar
  that raised the earth
  from the waters
  and let it flourish.

Knowing that it is only one
  of your Acts,
we know no one really can know
  the true age
  of your antiquity.

First One, Lord of the Wheel,
  we bow,
  we sing your praise.

2. How You Appear

O you, you appear young
to those who say
you're younger,
and brother to the conch-colored one.

To those who say
you're older,
and brother to the one dressed
in clothes dark as all-burying darkness
with a gold palmyra for banner,
you appear older.

To the undying wisdom
sifted without error
by sages
you appear in a state
of neither-nor.

Yet in any search
for true awareness
in this state or that,
you show only your own,
the excellence
of your most ancient state.

3. The Red Goddess

Wearing jewels
many-colored as rainbows
   bent across the high heavens
on your chest, itself a jewel
studded with pendant pearls,
you always wear the Red Goddess
as the moon wears
his shadow.
                    Which doesn't agree at all
with those who read the Vedas
and say,

            You as the Boar,
with white tusks, sharp and spotted,
washed by the rising waves,
you lifted up and married
the Earth-maiden,

so not a spot of earth
is ever troubled by the sea.

4. The Lord at War

Lord fierce in war,
the conch you blow
sounds like thunder
to the enemies
rising as one man,

hearts raging, fearless,
rising like a hurricane
to join battle.

Banners break and fall,
ears go deaf,
crowns shiver on their heads,
and the earth loosens
under their feet
at the thunder of your conch.

O lord fierce in war,
the discus in your hand
cuts off the sweet lives
of enemies:
heads fall and roll
wreaths and all
like tens of thousands
of bunches
on the heads of tall black palmyra trees
not stripped yet
of root, branch,
frond, or young fruit,
falling to the earth
all at once.

Not one head
standing on its body,
beheaded all at one stroke,
they gather, roll, split,
come together and roll apart,
and lie dead at last
in a mire of blood.

That discus
consumes enemies at one stroke:
Death is its body,
its color the leaping flame

of bright fire
when gold burns in it.

5. *His Forms*

Yours is the luster
of the great blue sapphire;

your eyes, a pair
of famed lotuses;

the truth of your word
certain as the returning day.

If one looks for your patience
it's there, magnificent, wide as earth;

your grace,
a sky of raincloud
fulfilling everyone;

so say the sacred texts
of the eloquent brahmans.

O lord with the red-beaked
Garuḍa-bird
on your banner,

you're like all that
and also like all else, and beyond,

you're in these,
and in all things everywhere:

> in the sacrificer's
> Vedic word,
>
> in the sacrificial pillar
> built step by step,

and also in the seizing
of the sacrificial animal
strapped to that pillar,

the kindling of a raging fire
according to charted text
and famous tradition,

and in the building of that fire
to glowing light
and prosperous flame

is your form,
your food:

in all these
brahmans see
your presence
that composes even aliens
who doubt your presence.

In your heart
you had only to think
ambrosia,
food of the gods,
and the gods received at once
life without age,
peace without end.

Lord unfathomable,
at your feet
we bow,
clean of heart,
putting our heads to the ground
over and over
we bow,
we praise,
we celebrate,

and we ask, O lord,
with our dear ones around us
we ask:

may our knowing
know
only what is.

Kīrantaiyār
Paripāṭal 2

Murukaṉ, the Red One
His Dances

The possessed shaman with the spear
wears wreaths of green leaves
   with aromatic nuts between them
and beautiful long pepper,
   wild jasmine and the three-lobed
      white nightshade.

His jungle tribes
   have chests bright with sandal;
the strong-bowed warriors
   in their mountain village
drink with their kin
sweet liquor, honey brew
   aged in long bamboos,
they dance rough dances
   hand in hand
      to the beat of small
         hillside drums.

The women
wear wreaths of buds
   fingered and forced to blossom
      so they smell differently,
wear garlands
   from the pools on the hill
      all woven into chains,

cannabis leaves
   in their dense hair,

white clusters
   from a sacred cadamba tree
   red-trunked and flowering,

arrayed between large cool leaves
  for the male beetle to suck at,

in leaf-skirts
  shaking
  on their jeweled mounds of love,

and their gait sways with the innocence
  of peacocks.

The shaman
is the Red One himself,
is in red robes;
young leaves of the red-trunk *aśoka*
flutter in his ears;

he wears a coat of mail,
  a warrior band on his ankle,
    a wreath of scarlet ixora;

has a flute,
  a horn,
  several small instruments
  of music;

for vehicles
  he has a ram,
  a peacock;

a faultless rooster
  on his banner;

the Tall One
  with bracelets on his arms,

with a bevy of girls, voices
like lute-strings,

a cloth
cool-looking above the waistband
tied so it hangs
all the way to the ground,

his hands large
as drumheads
hold gently
several soft-shouldered
fawnlike women;

he gives them proper places
and he dances
on the hills:

and all such things happen
because
of His being
there.

And not only there.

Nakkīraṉār
Tirumurukāṟṟuppaṭai:5
('A Guide to Lord Murukaṉ')

AFTERWORD

203. அன்னாய் வாழிவேண் டன்னை நம் படப்பைத்
தேன்மயங்கு பாலினு மினிய வவர்நாட்
டுவலைக் கூவற் கீழ
மானுண் டெஞ்சிய கலிழி நீரே.

எ - து உடன்போய் மீண்ட தலைமகள், 'நீ சென்றநாட்டு நீர் இனியவல்ல; நீ எங்ஙனம் [1] நுகர்ந்தாய்?' எனக்கேட்ட தோழிக்குக் கூறியது.

குறிப்பு. படப்பைத்தேன் - தோட்டக்கூற்றிலுள்ள தேன். மயங்கு பாலினும் இனிய - கலந்த பாலைக்காட்டிலும் இனிமைபொருந்தியன. உவலைக் கூவற்கீழ - தழையையுடைய கிணற்றின் அடியிலுள்ள : உவலை - தழை. தழைமூடிய எனலுமாம். மான் - மிருகங்கள். கலிழிநீர் - கலங்கல் நீர். மானுண்டெஞ்சிய நீரையுண்ணுதல்: குறுந். 56 : 1-3. அவர் நாட்டுக் கலிழி நீர் பாலினும் இனிய.

(மேற்.) மு. உடன்போய் மீண்ட தலைவி நீ சென்ற நாட்டு நீர் இனியவல்ல எங்ஙனம் நுகர்ந்தாயென்ற தோழிக்குக் கூறியது (தொல். அகத். 43, ந.) (பி - ம்.) [1] 'நுகர்ந்தவாறெனக்' (ரு.)

Text of Aiṅkuṟunūṟu 203 ("Sweeter than milk"), with commentary

In this afterword,[1] I shall offer readings of a number of poems, comment on the special ways these poems are made, the way they move, the figures they make; outline a certain world picture they create and share; relate the poetry to Tamil poetics and its key terms, *akam* and *puṟam*.

The oldest Tamil work on grammar and poetics, the *Tolkāppiyam*, suggests these succinctly in a few hundred aphorisms. My readings are indebted to that text and its many commentators as well as to the commentaries on the poems. In translating (or reading) an ancient Tamil poem, one is translating a poem, a tradition of commentary, and one's current sense of both.

Two Poems

One of the first poems in this book goes like this:

What She Said
to her girl friend, when she returned
from the hills

Bless you, friend. Listen.
Sweeter than milk
mixed with honey from our gardens
is the leftover water in his land,
low in the waterholes
covered with leaves
and muddied by animals.

Kapilar
Aiṅkuṟuṉūṟu 203

The speaker in the poem begins with a greeting to her girl friend, talks about the familiar and safe childhood drink of milk and garden honey, and moves delightedly to her lover's wilder, dirtier, animal-ridden waterholes. It is a poem about her first sexual experience, her growing up, her discovery that leaf-covered waterholes are more fascinating than domestic milk and honey. She is leaving behind order, cultivation, culture, milk and honey, to drink of the waters of nature, sharing it with the animals who muddy it. The Tamil original[2] opens with the greeting word *aṉṉāy* which means "mother," or any kinswoman, here her girl friend; it ends with *kaḻili nīrē*, "the muddied water." It moves from the maternal bosom into the sexual world of her man. The two places, her garden and his land, describe two states, and also two kinds of people. The man's land is like the man himself. From another angle, the speaker herself is the waterhole and he is the happy animal; and she is delighted. Thus a simple short piece says many things, as we dwell on it.

No names of persons or places appear in such poems. In the moment of experience, there is no society. The lovers are a solitude in the hills.

Yet there are characters, a family, around the lovers. The title (given by the colophons and expanded by the commentators), and the other poems with similar motifs, frame the moment. This poem is one of a group of ten, which itself belongs to a larger series of poems on the theme of lovers' meetings, set in the hillside.

Some of the poems are meant to be overheard by the mother or the lover, so that they will know what she is thinking and feeling. So the speech in the poem often has ulterior motives; it is a multiple utterance.

The speaker seems to be half talking to herself, yet addressing a confidante. It is like a speech in a play. The speaker is not the poet, Kapilar, but a persona; the poems, with their given titles and situations, carry the entire context within them (who said what to whom, when and why). An experienced Tamil reader would recognize such a poem as an *akam* poem. The meanings of *akam*, "interior, heart, household," are all embodied here.

A *puṟam* poem is very different. *Puṟam* means "exterior, outer parts of the body, yard outside the house, public."

King Kiḷḷi in Combat

With the festival hour close at hand,
his woman in labor,
a sun setting behind pouring rains,

the needle in the cobbler's hand
is in a frenzy
stitching thongs for a cot:

swifter, far swifter,
were the tackles of our lord
wearing garlands of laburnum,

as he wrestled with the enemy
come all the way
to take the land.

Cāttantaiyār: on Pōrvaikkōp-
perunar Kiḷḷi
Puṟanāṉūṟu 82

In this poem, the theme is war. We know the names of the combatants. According to the colophon, it describes a wrestling contest between Peruṉar Kiḷḷi (the Cōḻa king) and Mūkkavaṉāṭṭu Āmūr Mallaṉ. Legend says that the match could have lost Kiḷḷi his kingdom, for that was the wager. Thus the poem, unlike the *akam* poem, is associated with a real place, a time, an event of history.

The first part of the poem describes a low-born cobbler's haste and skill as he races against time—the sun is setting, the festival hour approaching, his woman is in labor, and he has to finish a cot for his wife's lying-in. (Tamil custom, to this day, requires that a woman give birth on a cot.) He must finish before the light fails. As an ancient commentator, Pērāciriyar, points out, all these images are related directly to the skillful moves of a Cōḻa king. The cobbler's urgency is not less than the king's. When the cobbler finishes his anxious task, if he succeeds in time, his wife's labor will end in childbirth, and a festival will begin. When the king wins, the land will be reborn, the enemy routed, and there will be much rejoicing. The two ends of society, the cobbler and the king, are one in this enterprise. The poem, by its syntax and the comparison, makes them one: the festival, the sunset, and the woman in labor qualify the cobbler's needle, which in turn describes the king's movements in combat. In *puṟam* poems, as we shall see, the whole society, beginning with the lowest born, is engaged in the action of the hero, contributes in a chain of works (as enacted by the phrases of this poem) to the king's success in war. In one interpretation, the cobbler is making a cot for the king. The cobbler enters the poem not merely to serve as metaphor. He exists in his own right, he occupies half the poem; the king is like him, they coexist, his energies move the limbs of the royal hero.

Furthermore, the flower in the poem is only the emblem of a clan, not a figure as it would be in an *akam* poem, occupying the center of the action, as part of the poetic enactment (e.g., the waterholes in the first poem). The *puṟam* poem is spoken by the poet himself; the *akam* poem through a persona, the woman in love.

Thus, the two genres differ from each other in theme as well as in rhetoric. And, as we shall see, they have also many things in common, inhabit the same world.

Akam and Puṟam

Akam and *puṟam* are ancient, complex words. To understand them is to enter Tamil poetics, and much that is crucial to Tamil culture. According to *A Dravidian Etymological Dictionary*, they are also current in all the South Dravidian languages and in Telugu and Tulu. In classical poetry, as we have seen, *akam* poems are love poems; *puṟam* are all other kinds of poems, usually about war, values, community; it is the "public" poetry of the ancient Tamils, celebrating the ferocity and glory of kings, lamenting the death of heroes, the poverty of poets. Elegies, panegyrics, invectives, poems on wars and tragic events are *puṟam* poems.

The *Tolkāppiyam* distinguishes *akam* and *puṟam* as follows:

> In [the five phases of] *akam*, no names of persons should be mentioned. Particular names are appropriate only in *puṟam* poetry.
>
> (*Tol.* 57)

The dramatis personae for *akam* are types, such as men and women in love, foster-mothers, girl friends, etc., rather than historical persons. Similarly, landscapes are more important than particular places. The reason for such absence of individuals is implicit in the word *akam*: the "interior" world is archetypal, it has no history, and no names of persons and places, except, now and then, in its metaphors. Love in all its variety (with important exceptions)—love in separation and in union, before and after marriage, in chastity and in betrayal—is the theme of *akam*.

> There are seven types of love, of which the first is *kaikkiḷai* or unrequited love, and the last is *peruntiṇai* or mismatched love.
>
> (*Tol.* 1)

Peruntiṇai, or the "major type" (as the *Tolkāppiyam* somewhat cynically calls it), of man-woman relationship is the forced loveless relationship: a man and a woman, mismatched in age, coming together for duty, convenience, or lust. At the other extreme is *kaikkiḷai* (literally, the "base relationship"), the one-sided affair, unrequited love, or desire inflicted on an immature girl who does not understand it. Neither of these extremes is the proper subject of *akam* poetry. They are common, abnormal, undignified, fit only for servants.

> Servants and workmen are outside the five *akam* types [of true love], for they do not have the necessary strength of character.
> (*Tol.* 25–26)

Most of the *akam* anthologies contain no poems of unrequited or mismatched love; only *Kalittokai* (e.g., "The Hunchback and the Dwarf," discussed below) has examples of both types. They follow none of the formal constraints on theme and structure that are characteristic of the *akam* poems.

Of the seven types, only the middle five are the subject of true love poetry. The hero and heroine should be "well-matched in ten points" such as beauty, wealth, age, virtue, rank, etc. Only such a pair is capable of the full range of love: union and separation, anxiety, patience, betrayal, forgiveness. The couple must be cultured; for the uncultured will be rash, ignorant, self-centered, and therefore unfit for *akam* poetry.

The Five Landscapes

The *Tolkāppiyam* opens its outline of *akam* poetics with a statement about the world of the poems:

When we examine the materials of a poem, only three things appear to be important: *mutal* [the "first things," i.e., time and place], *karu* [the "native elements"], and *uri* [the "human feelings" appropriately set in *mutal* and *karu*].

(*Tol.* 3)

"Place" is first divided into four kinds of regions, which are constituted by combinations of the five elements, earth, water, air, fire, sky (or space). Each region is presided over by a deity and named after a characteristic flower or tree:

mullai, a variety of jasmine, represents the forests overseen by *Māyōṉ*, "the Dark One," the dark-bodied god of herdsmen [*Viṣṇu*];

kuṟiñci, a mountain flower, stands for the mountains overseen by *Cēyōṉ*, "the Red One," *Murukaṉ*, the red-speared god of war, youth, and beauty;

marutam, a tree with red flowers growing near the water, for the pastoral region overseen by *Vēntaṉ*, "King," identified with the rain god [Indra];

neytal, a water flower, for the sandy seashore overseen by *Varuṇan*, the wind god.

(*Tol.* 5)

A rather special fifth region, *pālai* or desert waste, is overseen by *Koṟṟavai*, a demonic goddess of war, according to later writers. *Pālai* is supposedly a green desert tree that is unaffected by drought. *Pālai* has no specific location, for it is thought that any mountain or forest may be parched to a wasteland in the heat of summer.[3]

Time is divided into day, month, and year. The year is divided into six "large time units," the six seasons: the rains (August–September), the cool season (October–November), the season of evening dew (December–January), the season of morning dew (February–March), early summer (April–May), and late summer (June–July). The day is divided into five "small time units": morning, midday, evening, nightfall, the dead of night. Some would add a sixth, dawn.

Particular "large time units" and "small time units" are associated by convention with particular regions.

Mullai country is associated with the rainy season and evening;
kuṟiñci, with the season of evening dew and midnight;
marutam, with the later part of night and the dawn;
neytal with the twilight or evening;
pālai with summer, the season of morning dew, and midday.
(*Tol.* 6–12)

Each of the five regions or landscapes is associated further with an appropriate *uri* or phase of love. (The phases of war are discussed below.)

Lovers' union is associated with *kuṟiñci*, the mountain;
separation with *pālai*, the desert;
patient waiting, with *mullai*, the forests;
anxious waiting, with *neytal*, the seashore;
the lover's infidelity and the beloved's resentment, with *marutam*, the cultivated agricultural region or lowland.
(*Tol.* 16)

Of these five, the first is clandestine (*kaḷavu*), before marriage; the fifth occurs after marriage. The other three could be either before or after marriage. *Pālai*, separation, includes not only the hardships of the lover away from his love, his search for wealth, fame, and learning, but also the elopment of the couple, their hardships on the way, and their separation from their parents.

We may note a few features of the native categories of the Tamil system. First things (time and place) and native elements are distinguished from *uri* (appropriate human feelings and experience); the systematic symbology depends on the association between these two sets. They are distinct, yet co-present. They require each other; together they make the world. *Mutal* and *karu*, first things and native elements, are seen as the "objective correlatives," or rather the correlative objects,[4] of human experience. It is also significant that, in this Tamil system, though gods are mentioned, they are only part of the scene; they preside, but as natives of the landscape.[5] There seems to be no creator-creature relation in the early anthologies.

In the *karu*, "things born into, or native to, a region," no clear distinction is made between nature and culture; among the native elements of a landscape are listed flora, fauna, tribes as well as arts, styles, instruments. Furthermore, the *Tolkāppiyam* (582 ff.) considers all native elements, especially all animate beings, as part of a continuous series[6] graded by degrees of sentience:

Things without any sentience: stones, water, etc.
Beings with one sense (touch):
grass, trees, creepers
Beings with two senses (touch and taste):
snails, shellfish
Beings with three senses (touch, taste, smell):
termites, ants
Beings with four senses (touch, taste, smell, vision):
crabs, lobsters, beetles, bees
Beings with five senses (touch, taste, smell, vision, hearing):
birds, beasts, and uncultured people
Beings with six senses (touch, taste, smell, vision, hearing, mind): human beings and gods.

In poetry, says the *Tolkāppiyam*, the above categories are both used and crossed, say, in figures like metaphor and personification. Time may become a winged bird, a bird may be seen as a messenger of love, and love may be felt as a river in flood. As some philosophers would say, a metaphor is a "category mistake." A special figure (called *bhrānti-madalaṅkāra* in Sanskrit) depends on one thing being mistaken for another. George Hart (1975:275–77) discusses this figure and points out that, historically speaking, it occurs first in Tamil and later in Sanskrit poetry. Here is a Tamil example:

What Her Girl Friend Said to Her

These fat cassia trees
are gullible:

the season of rains
that he spoke of
when he went through the stones
of the desert
is not yet here

though these trees
mistaking the untimely rains
have put out
long arrangements of flowers
on their twigs

as if for a proper monsoon.

Kōvatattaṉ,
Kuṟuntokai 66

The heroine is waiting for her lover's return; he has promised to return by the first rains. Cassia trees usually flower at that time and signal the season of rains. Here the girl friend is asking the heroine to be patient—not to be mindless and deluded like the cassia trees. Trees have only one sense (touch) and mistake an untimely sprinkle for the real monsoon. The woman should use her other senses, not make the same mistake.

Such a figure always involves animals (which lack mind, the sixth sense), or plants (which have only one sense), as in the above poem. This way of thinking prevents the use of some well-known figures of speech. For instance, the kind of "pathetic fallacy" that directly attributes mind to animals and objects is quite rare in Tamil poetry (except in ironic contexts, or where the speaker is overwhelmed by feeling). However, animal behavior may suggest human behavior, by parallels and contrasts, to the human witnesses; for only human beings have the sixth sense to see such parallels, their poetry, and their irony.

According to both the Indian and the Western traditions, every sign is a union of signifier and signified (e.g., Saussure 1959:65–67). In the Tamil system of correspondences, a whole language of signs is created by relating the landscapes as signifiers to the *uri* or appropriate human feelings.

In this world of correspondences between times, places, things born in them, and human experiences, a word like *kuṟiñci* has several concentric circles of meaning: a flower, the mountain landscape, lovers' union, a type of poem about all these, and musical modes for these poems. But its concrete meaning, "a mountain flower" is never quite forgotten.

A conventional design thus provides a live vocabulary of symbols; the actual objective landscapes of Tamil country become the interior landscapes of Tamil poetry. Chart 1 tabulates some of these features. It would be useful, initially at least, to refer to the list of symbols when reading the poems.

The *Tolkāppiyam* takes care to add that "birds and beasts of one landscape may sometimes appear in others": artful poets may work with an "overlap of genres" *(tiṇai-mayakkam);* they may even bring in war imagery to heighten the effects of an *akam* poem. The *Tolkāppiyam* further states that the above genres are not rigidly separated; the time and

Chart 1. Some Features of the Five Landscapes

	LOVERS' UNION	PATIENT WAITING, DOMESTICITY	LOVER'S UNFAITHFULNESS, "SULKING SCENES"	ANXIETY IN LOVE, SEPARATION	ELOPEMENT, HARDSHIP, SEPARATION FROM LOVER OR PARENTS
Characteristic flower (name of region and poetic genre)	*kuṟiñci*	*mullai* (jasmine)	*marutam* (queen's-flower)	*neytal* (blue lily)	*pālai* (desert tree)
Landscape	mountains	forest, pasture	countryside, agricultural lowland	seashore	wasteland (mountain or forest parched by summer)
Time	night	late evening	morning	nightfall	midday
Season	cool season, season of morning dew	rainy season	all seasons	all seasons	season of evening dew, summer
Bird	peacock, parrot	sparrow, jungle hen	stork, heron	seagull	dove, eagle
Beast (including fish, reptile, etc.)	monkey, elephant, horse, bull	deer	buffalo freshwater fish	crocodile shark	fatigued elephant, tiger, or wolf lizard
Tree or plant	jackfruit, bamboo, *vēṅkai* (kino)	*koṉṟai* (cassia)	mango	*puṉṉai* (laurel)	*ōmai* (toothbrush tree), cactus
Water	waterfall	rivers	pool	wells	waterless wells, stagnant water
Occupation or people	hill tribes, guarding millet harvest, gathering honey	plowman	pastoral occupations	selling fish and salt, fisherfolk	wayfarers, bandits

This is not an exhaustive list; only a few of the elements that appear frequently in the poems are given here. The Tamil names of gods, heroes, clans, musical instruments, and kinds of food have been omitted.

This chart first appeared in *The Interior Landscape* (Ramanujan 1967). For a more complete table, see Singaravelu (1966:22), or Zvelebil (1973:100)

place appropriate to one genre may be fused with the time and place appropriate to another:

> Anything other than *uri* or the appropriate mood may be fused or transformed.
>
> (*Tol.* 15)

The following poem is a good example of this mixture of landscapes.

What She Said

The bare root of the bean is pink
like the leg of a jungle hen,
and herds of deer attack its overripe pods.

For the harshness
of this season of morning dew
there is no cure

but the breast of my man.

Aḷḷūr Naṉmullai
Kuruntokai 68

The season is morning dew (*kuṟiñci*), but the bird mentioned is a jungle hen (*mullai*), the beast is a deer (*mullai*). The mixture of *kuṟiñci* (lovers' union) and *mullai* (patient waiting) brings out effectively the exact nuance of the girl's mood, "mixing memory and desire" in a kind of montage.

Thus, for poetry, the hierarchy of components is inverted; the human elements (*uri*), the native elements (*karu*), and the first elements (*mutal*) are in a descending order of importance for a poet. Mere nature description or imagism in poetry would be uninteresting to classical Tamil poets and critics, for it would not "signify"; it would be a signifier without a signified, a landscape (*mutal* and *karu*) without an *uri*, an appropriate human mood.

Poetic Design

The conventions make for many kinds of economy in poetic design. Consider the following poem:

What She Said

Bigger than earth, certainly,
higher than the sky,
more unfathomable than the waters
is this love for this man

of the mountain slopes
where bees make rich honey
from the flowers of the *kuṟiñci*
that has such black stalks.

Tēvakulattār
Kuṟuntokai 3

The *kuṟiñci* flower and the mountain scene clearly mark this as a *kuṟiñci* poem about lovers' union. The union is not described or talked about; it is enacted by the "inset" scene of the bees making honey from the flowers of the *kuṟiñci*. The lover is not only the lord of the mountain; he is *like* the mountain he owns. Describing the scene describes his passion. The *kuṟiñci*, being a plant that takes about twelve years to come to flower, carries a suggestion assimilating the tree to the young tropical heroine who speaks the poem. The *Tolkāppiyam* calls this technique of using the scene to describe act or agent, *uḷḷuṟai uvamam*, hidden or implicit metaphor.

Furthermore, the poem opens with large abstractions about her love: her love is bigger than earth and higher than the sky. But it moves toward the concreteness of the black-stalked *kuṟiñci*, acting out by analogue the virgin's progress from abstraction to experience. We may remember that this progression (from the basic cosmic elements to the specific component of a landscape) is also the method of the entire intellectual framework behind the poetry: moving from first elements to native elements to human feelings. The poem in the original opens with earth, sky, and water, moves through the native elements of the mountain landscape (slopes, bees, *kuṟiñci*) and ends with a human feeling, *naṭpu*, "love."

Evocations designed like these may be seen in poem after poem. *Uḷḷuṟais*—let us call them insets—of the natural scene (somewhat like G. M. Hopkins's inscape) repeat the total action of the poem. Here are two clear examples from a sequence:

What She Said

In his place, mother,

mud-spattered spotted crabs
sneak into holes at the root
of the nightshade.

O what's the point
of his marrying me then
with sweet talk,
and saying
these other things now?

In his country,

spotted crabs
born in their mother's death
grow up with crocodiles
that devour their young.

Why is he here now?

And why does he
take those women,

a jangle of gold bangles
as they make love,

only to leave them?

Ōrampōkiyār
Aiṅkuṟunūṟu 22, 24

These are *marutam* poems, poems about infidelity, set in the fertile, well-watered countryside. In the first, he has done to her what the crabs do to the nightshade—sneaked into the hole and gnawed at the root. In the second, the spotted crabs and crocodiles of his region, cannibals all, kill and eat the dear kin they ought to love and protect—like the man himself.

Metaphor and Metonymy

A word about the theory of *uḷḷuṟai uvamam* or insets. An inset is an implicit comparison. All explicit markers of comparison are suppressed. The *Tolkāppiyam* says that explicit comparison belongs to worldly usage *(ulakavaḻakku)*, whereas implicit metaphor belongs to poetic usage *(ceyyuḷvaḻakku)*.

There are other distinctions to be made. (a) An inset is a correlation of the landscapes and their contents *(karu)* to the human scene *(uri)*. (b) Unlike metaphor in ordinary language, an inset is a structural feature within the poem; it integrates the different elements of the poem and shapes its message. (c) Unlike metaphor and simile, it often leaves out all the points of comparison and all explicit markers of comparison (e.g., "like," "as"); such an omission increases manyfold the power of the figure. As we have seen in the poems, image intensifies image, associations flow into each other. These "montage" and "dissolve" effects are aided by the flowing syntax of the language. (d) The inset is essentially a "metonymy,"[7] an *in presentia* relationship, where both terms are present, where the signifier and the signified belong to the same universe, share the same "landscape." Both are parts of one scene. Such a metonymy, rather than metaphor, is the favorite poetic figure of the classical Tamils. Metaphor implies diversity ("seeing similars in dissimilars" said Aristotle), to be unified by comparison. Poetry for the Tamils does not unify a *multiverse* but expresses a universe from within, speaking through any of its parts. The man belongs to the scene, the scene represents the man. Adapting a remark of Kenneth Burke's (1945:6–7) in another context, we may say, "There is implicit in the quality of a scene the quality of the action implicit in it . . . one could deduce the details of the action from the details of the setting." This kind of "metonymous metaphor," based on an entire formal scheme, is a special feature of classical Tamil forms.

But then complex insets are not used everywhere in the poems; they are specifically preferred in the most structured of Tamil poetic genres—the fivefold *akam;* they are not used in the *peruntiṇai* (the mismatched affair), nor preferred in the heroic *puṟam* poems.

The Tamil theory of comparison deserves an essay to itself. I shall content myself here with only one more feature. All comparisons, says the *Tolkāppiyam* (276), whether explicit or implicit, involve terms of comparison. These terms may refer to shape, color, action, or result. Examples abound in the poems I have quoted. Like the comparisons between crab and lover, that between cobbler and king (p. 233) is based on *action;* when the bare root of the bean is pink like the leg of a jungle hen, the points of comparison are *color* and *shape.* If we consider color and shape as special cases of sensory attributes in general, we can include comparisons based on touch, taste, etc., which occur in the poems, e.g., "sweeter than milk and honey." Of course, through color, shape, action, and result, these comparisons convey much more. Usually, several terms are present in any comparison. For instance, in the poem at the beginning of the last section (p. 244), the emphasis is on the *action* of the bee and the *resulting* honey. The *shapes* of the flower and the bee also suggest obvious sexual images.

The Personae

The *dramatis personae* in *akam* poems are limited to a small number: the hero, the heroine, the hero's friend(s) or messengers, the heroine's friend and foster-mother, the concubine, and passersby. In the *puṟam* poems, the poets mostly speak in their own person, though there are a few exceptions.

No *akam* poet speaks in his own voice; and no poem is addressed to a reader. The reader only overhears what the characters say to each other or to themselves or to the moon. A poem in this tradition implies, evokes, enacts a drama in a monologue.

The situations *(tuṟai)* when a hero or heroine or one of their companions may speak out, and to whom, are closely defined. For example,

> The girl friend of the heroine may speak out on the following occasions: when the heroine, left behind by her lover, speaks of her loneliness; when she helps them elope; when she begs the hero to take good care of the heroine; when she tries to dissuade the parents from their search for the runaway couple, or consoles the grieving mother . . .
>
> (Tol. 42)

An interesting convention usually restricts the imagery for different speakers within the poems. The heroine's images are mostly confined to what surrounds her house, or to the wonder of discovering his landscape or to hearsay and fantasies about it. The concubine or the heroine's girl friend or foster-mother have more ranging images: they are of a lower class, and their experience is wider. The man's imagery has even greater range. Apparently there are no limits to his experience, and therefore to his imagery. Thus the range of imagery, its quality or content, its very narrowness or width of choice, indirectly characterizes speaker and social class.

The Two Proprieties

The *Tolkāppiyam* speaks of "two kinds of proprieties: those of drama and those of the world." The conventional proprieties outlined so far are of the mode of drama. The situations of real life in the real world are governed by another set of proprieties. The strategy of the poet is to deploy both, to keep the tension between the forms of art and the forms of the world.

A highly formal scheme of landscapes that have neither name nor history bears within it the real land, the vivid particulars of bird, beast, insect, drumbeat, and waterfall.

A little-known book in Tamil by a botanist (Cāmi 1967; see also Varadarajan 1969) documents one's constant sense that these poets knew their fauna and flora: their botanical observations, for instance, are breathtakingly minute and accurate. In these poems, over two hundred plants of all the five Tamil regions are named, described, used in insets and comparisons. Root, stem, bark, bud, petal, inflorescence, seasons, special kinds of pollination, etc., are observed and alluded to. And their properties are aptly used to evoke human relationships.

We may ask, as the Tamil commentators do, why did

the poets pick the *kuṟiñci* as the one flower that will name the mountain landscape and the mood of first love? Though such signs are symbols, cultural assignments, arbitrary conventions, they are half-motivated by botanical facts: the *kuṟiñci* plant, of the *Strobilanthes* genus, grows only 6,000 feet above sea level; so it is the mountain flower par excellence. Botanical calendars kept for over a century on South Indian hills like the Nilgiris show that a *kuṟiñci* plant comes to flower only from nine to twelve years after it is planted—this identifies it with the tropical virgin heroine who comes to puberty at the same age.

Kuṟiñci plants flower all at once on the mountain slopes, covering them with millions of blossoms, certainly a great symbol for the suddenness and the overwhelming nature of first love. It is a "honey" flower, rich in honey. The bees that frequent it frequent no other, thus making what beekeepers call "unifloral honey," which is as rich as it is rare and pure. Furthermore, the *kuṟiñci* is fiercely competitive—it permits no other tree to grow in its neighborhood.

Thus is the real world always kept in sight and included in the symbolic. These poets would have made a modern poet like Marianne Moore (1951:41) happy: they are "literalists of the imagination," presenting for inspection in poem after poem "imaginary gardens with real toads in them."

A Language Within Language

In a sense, the tradition of conventions does everything possible to depersonalize the poetry of *akam*. It gives all that can be *given* to a poet, and makes of poetry a kind of second language.

The poet's language is not only Tamil: landscapes, the personae, the appropriate moods, all become a language within language. Like a native speaker he makes "infinite use of finite means," to say with familiar words what has never been said before; he can say exactly what he wants to, without even being aware of the ground rules of his grammar. If the world is the vocabulary of the poet, the conventions are his syntax—at least one of the many kinds of poetic syntax.

The lyric poet likes to find ways of saying many things while saying one thing; he would like to suggest an entire astronomy by his specks and flashes. Toward this end, the Tamil poets used a set of five landscapes and formalized the world into a symbolism. By a remarkable consensus, they all spoke this common language of symbols for some five or six generations. Each could make his own poem and by doing so allude to every other poem which had been, was being, or would be written in this symbolic language. Thus poem became relevant to poem, as if they were all written by a single hand. The spurious name *Caṅkam* ("Fraternity," "Community") for this poetry was justified not by history but by the poetic practice.

Puṟam Poetry

The language of *akam* is only half the story. The scheme should include the *puṟam* poems, as well as the mismatched and the one-sided love affairs that define by contrast the tight structure of the fivefold *akam*.

The *puṟam* poems correspond to the *akam* poems in many ways. The *Tolkāppiyam* finds a *puṟam* parallel for every one of the seven genres of *akam*. Six of them are named after a flower or a plant. For instance, *vākai*, the sirissa tree of the desert region, lends its name to the *puṟam* genre depicting ideals of achievement—parallel to it is *pālai* in love poetry, which depicts a lover going through the

Chart 2. *Puṟam/Akam* Correspondences

Akam	*Situation/Theme*	*Puṟam*	*Situation/Theme*	*Common Features*
1. *kuṟiñci*, a mountain flower	first union	*veṭci*, scarlet ixora	cattle-lifting, prelude to war	night, hillside; clandestine affair
2. *mullai*, jasmine	separation (patience)	*vañci*, a creeper	preparation for war, invasion	forest, rainy season; separation from loved ones
3. *marutam*, queen's flower	infidelity (conflict)	*uḻiñai*, a cotton shrub	siege	fertile area (city, etc.), dawn; refusing entry
4. *neytal*, water lily	separation (anxiety)	*tumpai*, white dead nettle	battle	seashore, open battle-ground, no season; evening; grief
5. *pālai*, desert tree	elopement, search for wealth, fame, etc.	*vākai*, sirissa tree	ideals of achievement, victory	no particular landscape; praise
6. *peruntiṇai*,[a] "major type"	mismatched love	*kāñci*, portia tree	struggle for excellence; endurance	no particular landscape; struggle
7. *kaikkiḷai*[a] "base relation"	unrequited love	*pāṭāṇ*,[a] "praise"	elegy, praise for heroes, asking for gifts, invective	no particular landscape; a one-sided relationship

[a] Not the name of a tree or a flower.

wilderness in search of wealth, fame, etc. Commentators elaborate on the correspondences further. Why should the *kuṟiñci* (union) phase of love correspond to *veṭci* (cattle raids) in war? Because, say the commentators, they both have to do with first encounters, are clandestine, take place at night on hillsides. Chart 2 displays one set of *akam/puṟam* correspondences.

Though these correspondences are in the rhetoric, however, they are not always active in the poetry. The landscapes are not consistently used as "insets," nor are the distinctions clear. The poem on the cobbler and the king, for instance, is considered a *vākai* poem (in praise of kings, etc.), and is a counterpart of *pālai* (desert: separation, hardship); but the images in the poem do not belong to the desert at all, but to the *mullai* (forest, pasture: waiting, marriage): rains, laburnum, evening, and childbirth. Of course, the colophon could be wrong, or wrongly transmitted, for the *mullai* images could fit very well with the parallel *vañci* (preparation for war). By and large, though, the *puṟam* divisions are not as clear as the ones in *akam*. For instance, the last two classes (*kāñci* and *pāṭāṇ*) are not clearly distinguished from the rest. *Pāṭāṇ* is a large mixed class, and does not bear the name of a tree or flower as the others do. Later writers add more separate classes, include in *puṟam* the classes of mismatched and unrequited love, and add a "general" class (*potunilai*) to make a twelvefold *puṟam*. By then only the "ideal fivefold," from *kuṟiñci* to *pālai*, is considered *akam*, "interior." Yet in reading *akam* and *puṟam* together one is struck as much by the common world they share as by the differences.

Whereas *akam* poems tend to focus on a single image, *puṟam* images rush and tumble over one another. Yet, as in the following *puṟam* poem, the same flowers and landscapes speak of war and peace, of fertility and desolation:

Where the Lilies Were in Flower

Fish leaping
in fields of cattle;

easy unplowed sowing
where the wild boar has rooted;

big-eyed buffalo herds
stopped by fences of lilies
flowering in sugarcane beds;

ancient cows bending their heads
over water flowers
scattered by the busy dancers
swaying with lifted hands;

queen's-flower trees full of bird cries,
the rustle of coconut trees,
canals from flowering pools
in countries
with cities sung in song:

> but your anger
> touched them, brought them terror,
> left their beauty in ruins,
> bodies consumed by Death.

The districts are empty, parched;
the waves of sugarcane blossom,
stalks of dry grass.
The thorny babul of the twisted fruit
neck to neck with the giant black babul.

The she-devil with the branching crest
roams
astraddle on her demon,
and the small persistent thorn
is spread in the moving dust
of ashen battlefields.

Not a sound, nothing animal,
not even dung,
in the ruins of public places
that kill the hearts of eager men,
chill all courage,
and shake those who remember.

But here,
the sages have sought your woods.
In your open spaces, the fighters play
with bright-jeweled women.
The traveler is safe on the highway.
Sellers of grain shelter their kin
who shelter, in turn, their kin.

The silver star will not go near
the place of the red planet: so it rains
on the thirsty fields.
Hunger has fled
and taken disease with her.

Great one,
your land blossoms
everywhere.

Kumaṭṭūr Kaṇṇaṉār:
on Imayavarampaṉ Neṭuñ-
cēralātaṉ
Patiṟṟupattu 13

The plant names are familiar: e.g., sugarcane, lilies, *marutam* or queen's-flower. The poem clearly falls into two parts, celebrating the destructive and protective functions of a king. The first part celebrates the fertility of the pastoral, agricultural, and seashore landscapes (cows, sugarcane, lilies, etc.); the middle part shows how they have been ravaged and turned into a *pālai* wilderness (the thorny babuls, etc.) by the war. The third section praises the king's own flourishing kingdom (forests and fields).

The *akam/puṟam* correspondences are not strict, but still close enough to allow us to integrate the two genres. Such correspondences should not be frozen into an exact taxonomy, for the Tamils never do so—they always make room for "overlap of classes" *(tiṇaimayakkam)* and "leftover classes" (e.g., *potunilai*).

Taken in the large, the two genres, poems of love and war—*akam* and *puṟam*—complement one another: contrasted in theme, mood, and structure but unified by imagery. Together, they make the classical, "bardic," Tamil world. This is why the same poets could write both *akam* and *puṟam* poems. Some poems explicitly place love and war together:

A Leaf in Love and War

The chaste trees, dark-clustered,
blend with the land
that knows no dryness;
the colors on the leaves
mob the eyes.

We've seen those leaves
on jeweled women,
on their mounds
of love.

Now the chaste wreath lies slashed
on the ground, so changed, so mixed
with blood, the vulture snatches it
with its beak,
thinking it raw meat.

We see this too
just because a young man

in love with war
wore it for glory.

Veṟipāṭiya Kāmakkaṇṇiyār
Puṟanāṉūṟu 271

The green leaves of the chaste tree were used as leaf-skirts by women and as laurels by warriors. So it is emblematic of *kuṟiñci* (union) in love and *uḻiñai* (battle) in war; the mere juxtaposition brings the irony home sharply.

One more contrast should be noticed. Though *akam* means "interior," *puṟam*, "exterior," *akam* poetry, which a modern reader might expect to be the most private and personal expression, is the most formally structured genre in the Tamil tradition; as we know, no names, individuals, or places are usually allowed here, only classes, ideal types; for in this inner world there are no names or individuals. *Puṟam*, the so-called "public poetry," is allowed names, places, expression of personal circumstances in a real society, a real history, and a certain freedom from the necessities of poetic convention both in insets and in the landscapes. Thus it is the "public" *puṟam* poetry that becomes the vehicle of personal expression and celebration of historical personages. Indeed, when a woman speaks in her own voice about her love, the poem is placed in a *puṟam* anthology (e.g., p. 119).

Love, Mismatched

Quite in contrast to both *akam* and *puṟam* genres as we have defined them stands the mismatched affair or *peruntiṇai*. Here is an example from *Kalittokai*, probably the latest of the eight anthologies.

The Hunchback and the Dwarf
A Dialogue

Hunchback woman,
the way you move is gentle
and crooked as a reflection
in the water,
                    what good deeds
did you do that I should want you so?

          O mother! (she swore to herself) Some
          auspicious moment made you dwarf,
          so tiny you're almost invisible,
          you whelp born to a man-faced owl,
          how dare you stop us to say
          you want us? Would such midgets
          ever get to touch such as us!

Lovely one,
                    curvaceous,
                              convex
as the blade of a plough,
you strike me with a love
I cannot bear.
                    I can live
only by your grace.

          (Look at this creature!)
          You dwarf, standing piece of timber,
          you've yet to learn the right approach
          to girls. In high noon
          you come to hold
          our hand and ask us to your place.
          Have you had any women?

Good woman,
                    your waist is higher

than your head, your face a stork,
plucked and skinned,
with a dagger for a beak,
                                        listen to me.
If I take you in the front, your hump
juts into my chest; if from the back
it'll tickle me in odd places.
                                        So I'll not
even try it. But come close anyway and let's touch
side to side.

> *Chi,* you're wicked. Get lost! You half-man!
> As creepers hang on only to the crook of a tree
> there are men who'd love to hold this hunch
> of a body close, though nothing fits. Yet, you lecher,
> you ask for us sideways. What's so wrong
> with us, you ball, you bush of a man.
> Is a gentle hunchback type far worse than a cake
> of black beans?

But I've fallen for you
(he said, and went after her).
O look, my heart,
at the dallying of this hunchback!

> Man, you stand
> like a creepy turtle stood up by somebody,
> hands flailing in your armpits.
> We've told you we're not for you. Yet you hang around.
> Look, he walks now like Kāma.

Yes, the love-god with arrows, brother to Cāma.
Look at this love-god!
                                        Come now, let's find joy,
you in me, me in you; come, let's ask and tell
which parts we touch.

I swear by the feet of my king.

All right, O gentle-breasted one. I too will give up
mockery.
            But I don't want this crowd in the palace
laughing at us, screaming when we do it,
"Hey, hey! Look at them mounting,
leaping like demon on demon!"

                                        O shape
of unbeaten gold, let's get away from the palace
to the wild jasmine bush. Come,
let's touch close, hug hard
and finish the unfinished,
then we'll be
like a gob of wax on a parchment
made out in a court full of wise men,
and stamped
to a seal.
            Let's go.

Marutaṉiḷanākaṉār
Kalittokai 94

Note the unheroic, even antiheroic, mock-heroic quality of this unlovely couple, looking not for love but frankly for sex; the folk-like bawdy, the earthy humor. There are no inset landscapes, though the poem is classified as *marutam*. Plows, herons, turtles, and wild jasmine jostle in it. In a single phrase like "You whelp born to a man-faced owl," many categories are undone. The piece makes comedy and poetry by violating over and over the decorum of *akam* poems. The metaphors are bold, explicit. The two persons are not even young—one of them is "a stork, plucked and skinned." This is *peruntiṇai*, the "major type," depicting the common human condition, love among the misfits with no scruples regarding the niceties of time or landscape; moving from mockery to coupling in the course of a conversation. Their misfit is evident even in their bodies' lack of fit. And they are obviously servants. We have also shifted from the dramatic monologues of *akam* and *puṟam* to dialogue and interaction, from lyric to comic drama. As in drama, the characters and their speech change: the hunchback begins with a royal *we* in her rejection and ends with an *I* in yielding; her mocking exclamations to herself drop off.

If the *akam* has the most tightly structured symbolic language, the *peruntiṇai* is free and realistic, with real toads in real cesspools.

We have not spoken of one genre: the *kaikkiḷai*, one-sided or unrequited love. There are not many classical examples of unrequited love. Here is one, from *Kuṟuntokai*:

What He Said

When love is ripe beyond bearing
and goes to seed,
men will ride even palmyra stems
as if they were horses;

will wear on their heads
the reeking cones of the *erukkam* bud
as if they were flowers;

will draw to themselves
the laughter of the streets;

and will do worse.

Pēreyiṉ Muruvalār
Kuṟuntokai 17

The most significant observation on *kaikkiḷai* (not found in the *Tolkāppiyam* but in later commentaries) is that such expression of one-sided love is appropriate only to religion. Postclassical Tamil devotees, preoccupied with their unrequited love for their god, in a cloud of unknowing, created the most poignant poems of *kaikkiḷai*.

Thus the four genres *(akam, peruntiṇai, kaikkiḷai,* and *puṟam)* cover and formalize the main possibilities of Tamil lyric poetry. They define each other mutually. A great deal of Western love poetry would probably be described by the ancient commentators as the one-sided *kaikkiḷai;* a great deal of modern poetry, fiction, and black comedy as love among the misfits or *peruntiṇai*—exploring the unheroic, the antiheroic, and presenting the ironies of impotence.

Poem becomes relevant to poem within the five *akam* landscapes and across the four genres as well.

Akam and Puṟam as Poetic Devices

Akam ("interior") and *puṟam* ("exterior") are not only thematic divisions. The paired opposition is pervasive in Tamil poetry and culture. The two key categories are related to each other by context and by contrast. The various meanings to be found in the *Tamil Lexicon* can be paired as follows:

	Akam	*Puṟam*
1.	interior	exterior
2.	heart, mind	body surfaces and extremities, e.g., back, side, arms
3.	self	others
4.	kin	non-kin
5.	house, family	houseyard, field
6.	inland, settlement	area far from dense human habitation, e.g., jungle, desert
7.	earth	farthest ocean
8.	love poems—no names of places or persons	poetry about war and other than (well-matched?) love, a "public" poetry, with names of real people and places
9.	Codes of conduct appropriate to *akam*	Codes of conduct appropriate to *puṟam*

The meanings complement each other systematically. As we move from context to context, for each meaning of *akam*, there is a corresponding sense of *puṟam*. It is characteristic of this poetry and its poetics that the meanings seem to expand and contract in concentric circles, with the concrete physical particular at the center, getting more and more inclusive and abstract as we move outward. The context picks and foregrounds one or another of these circles of meaning.

A poem moves along these various senses of *akam* and *puṟam:* this movement is one of the forms of the poem. In the course of such interplay, *akam/puṟam* contrasts such as inner/outer, self/other, nature/culture, household/wilderness become part of the form as well as the content of the poem.

For instance:

What He Said

In this long summer wilderness
  seized and devoured by wildfire,

if I should shut my eyes
  even a wink,

I see
  dead of night, a tall house
  in a cool yard, and the girl

with freckles
  like kino flowers,

hair flowing as with honey,
  her skin a young mango leaf.

Ōtalāntaiyār
Aiṅkuṟuṉūṟu 324

The poem consists of a number of movements from *puṟam* to *akam*, from the faraway wilderness to the inhabited house, from the outer landscape to the fantasy inside him; it also moves from the wildfire and noonday sun (*pā-lai,* desert, separation) to dead of night, the girl, the yellow kino flowers, and hair glistening as if with honey (all *ku-ṟiñci* images of lovers' union). Yet the whole poem stays with the *pālai* mood of a lover in a desert far away from his beloved.

Other subtleties should be noted: "seized and devoured by wildfire," an attribute of the outer wilderness, is also suggestive of the speaker's inner state. Where he is, is what he is: a scene/agent ratio (in Burke's terms), a metonymy, an *uḷḷuṟai*. He is contained by the wilderness devoured by wildfire; and he also contains it within him. But when he closes his eyes, he contains the house of his beloved in fantasy. We should also remember that *pālai* is one phase of a cycle—he is going away from his woman "for education, work, earning wealth, war"—all *puṟam* concerns. Among the relations between *akam* and *puṟam*, household and the world, one should include the rhythm of a man going out into the world and coming back into the family. Only a warrior who dies or an ascetic who renounces doesn't return—both are themes for *puṟam* poems. He passes through the *pālai* wilderness on his way to do "the world's work," and survives by remembering his home and woman, in the heat and wildfire of the outer desert and the inner. Of course, heat and wildfire for the separated lover have sexual overtones.

In reading these poems, one need not explicitly trace *akam/puṟam* shifts. They guide our responses subtly, surprising us often, by turning inside out. *Akam* and *puṟam* are part of the very choreography of poetic moves in Tamil poems. As one learns the "second language" of these poems, one also learns to sense the "ins and outs"; one follows the rhythms without labeling them, as one soon learns to read the language of cassias and tigers and waterfalls without running to a glossary of symbols.

Looked at in this way, each poem is a structure and a process. While *akam* and *puṟam*, and the five landscape genres, are opposed to each other as overall genres, and clearly defined as such, within each poem they work as phases, change points. One might even think of the action of each poem as a crossing of thresholds, across genres: the above *pālai* poem crosses from the outer landscape to the interior one, and also from the wilderness to the human settlement. Each of the genres enacts a characteristic crossing of the *akam/puṟam* oppositions.

Typically, the movement of *akam* poems is a crossing from outer to inner: from outer body to the heart within, in memory or imagination *(kuriñci);* from sea to land *(neytal),* from warfield to home *(mullai);* from home to wilderness in actuality, from wilderness to home in memory *(pālai);* from the concubine who is no kin, who lives on the town's outskirts, to home, wife, and kin *(marutam).*

Puṟam poems, like the following, tend to start inside a house *(akam)* and move, like the tiger, out into the world *(puṟam):*

> You stand against the pillar
> of my hut and ask:
>   Where is your son?
> I don't really know.
>
> My womb was once
> a lair
> for that tiger.
>
> You can see him now
> only in battlefields.
>
> Kāvaṟpeṇṭu
> *Puṟanāṉūṟu* 86

Often the poetic moment is actually poised on the threshold, though a figure in the poem may move (actually, or in imagination) from outer to inner. Many *marutam* poems are literally enacted at the door which is shut in the face of the unfaithful returning husband. The most extraordinary of these "door-shutting" *(vāyil maṟuttal)* poems moves from *puṟam* to *akam,* from the public realm of townsmen, kinsmen, and the wedding ceremony, step by step to the privacy of the bedroom and finally to the ultimate *akam* or "interior" of the bride's private parts:

What He Said

after a quarrel, remembering his wedding night

Serving in endless bounty
white rice and meat
cooked to a turn,
        drenched in ghee,
to honored guests,
and when the bird omens were right,
at the perfect junction
of the Wagon Stars with the moon
        shining in a wide soft-lit sky,

wedding site decorated, gods honored,
kettledrum and marriage drum
sounding loud the wedding beat,

the women who'd given her a bridal bath
—piercing eyes looking on, unwinking—
suddenly gone,

her near kin
strung a white thread on her
with the split soft-backed leaves
of the sirissa,
and with the *aruku* grass,

its sacred root a figurine,
its buds cool, fragrant,
dark-petaled, blue
as washed sapphire,

brought forth by the thundering skies
of first rains in valleys
where adolescent calves
feed on them,

they brought her to me
decked in new clothes,
rousing my desire
even in the wedding canopy,
wedding noises noisy as pounding rain,

on that first night,

and when they wiped her sweat,
and gave her to me,
she splendid with ornament,
I said to her

who was body now to my breath,
chaste without harshness,
wrapped all over in a robe
new, uncrushed,

"It's hot. Sweat is breaking out
on that crescent, your brow.
Open your robe a little,
let the wind cool it,"

and even as I spoke,
my heart hasty with desire,
I pulled it off

and she stood exposed,
her form shining
like a sword unsheathed,
not knowing how to hide herself,

cried *Woy!*
in shame, then bowed, begged of me,
as she loosened her hair
undoing the thick colorful wreath
of broken lily petals
and, with the darkness of black full tresses,
hand-picked flowers on them
still luring the bees,
hid
her private
parts.

Viṟṟūṟṟu Mūteyiṉaṉār
Akanāṉūṟu 136

Before we leave the manifold of *akam/puṟam,* we must note some more ways in which the two genres differ. Only the full cycle of love between well-matched lovers is called *akam;* all else, including ill-matched love, the life and death of heroes, their relations to land, clan, enemy, and bard, were called *puṟam*. The Tamil world was divided between family, or "household" (one meaning of *akam*) and the "kingdom," the outer world. Women were central to the former, as heroes (named kings and chieftains and unnamed warriors) were central to the latter. In an *akam* anthology like *Kuṟuntokai,* only 62 poems are assigned to the man, but 180 to the woman, 140 to her girl friend, 14 others to women characters like foster-mothers and concubines. In a *puṟam* anthology like *Puṟanāṉūṟu*, hardly a handful are spoken by women—about 18 songs are about or by women characters, mothers, wives, or widows of heroes. I am not counting the songs by women poets, such as the 13 by Auvaiyār (e.g., *Puṟanāṉūṟu* 101–4), which she sings not as a woman but as a bard about her patron.

In many *akam* poems, a woman's body is suggestively

present to our senses—the smell or texture of her hair, the shape of her breast, her brow, her mound of love or black-snake pubis, her leaf-skirts, the conch-shell bangles, her teeth like rice sprouts, her skin like young mango leaf, her great shoulders and red-streaked eyes, and in one poem even the taste of her saliva—yet a woman is never described in more than one or two details in each poem. We do not hear much about the man's appearance; we know more about what he has and about his country's scenery than about him. As we hear about her glittering bangles and ornaments, we also hear of his bright spear, his horses, chariots, garlands, ankle-bands, sometimes a chest enlarged by the drawing of bows. His spouse's chastity and virtue are also a chieftain's ornaments and his magical shields against disaster, as effective as his own "upright scepter" (*ceṅkōl,* as contrasted with *koṭuṅkōl* "crooked scepter"). It is significant that in the *akam* poems, rarely is the woman seen as the mature mother of a grown man, as she is in the *puṟam*. As in other heroic milieus, women bards, and poems in women's voices, enlist filial and familial feeling in the cause of war—especially that most compelling of family feelings, a mother's pride (or shame) about her son.

Techniques of Composition: Oral Poetics and Classical Tamil Poetry

I spoke earlier of a poetic "second language," the language of landscapes especially in *akam* poems. When we read *puṟam* poems, we are struck by another aspect of this second language, its repertoire of formulas, motifs, and such, which relates classical Tamil poetry to oral traditions.

The study of oral poetics,[8] especially the bardic technique of composition by theme and formula, has received much attention. V. Radlov, the pioneering Russian scholar who studied the Tartars of Central Asia in the 1890s, spoke of "elements of production" that bards of heroic poetry use in their improvisation. A bard composes, or recomposes, as he recites; he does not just reproduce a fixed narrative but produces new versions, sensitive to the needs and interests of a listening audience with whom he shares not only a mother tongue but a second language of poetry and narrative. Such elements of production may consist of themes, situations, catalogues, set pictures or topoi ("of the birth of a hero, of weapons, the story of battle, portraits of people and horses, the beauty of a bride"). "His art consists in piecing together these static components as circumstances require and connecting them with lines invented for the occasion." (Radlov, quoted in Kailasapathy 1968:135; see also Chadwick and Chadwick 1932–40:3:26). The Chadwicks (1932–40), in their three-volume survey of heroic poetry, surveyed Greek, Sanskrit, Celtic, Turkish, Pacific, and African sources and showed how universal such themes and techniques were in oral traditions. In the thirties, Milman Parry, somewhat extravagantly hailed as "the Darwin of Homeric studies," did pioneer studies of Homer and present-day Yugoslav bards; he showed how similar the Greek and the Yugoslav were in their "techniques of oral verse-making," in their ways of composing rapidly by skillful and various use of an art-language, a *Kunstsprache*, ready-made stock of formulas, formulaic systems (or patterns), themes, and type-scenes.[9] A. B. Lord's (1960) book *The Singer of Tales* continued Parry's work and has led to a series of studies in Anglo-Saxon, medieval French, and other epic narratives.

Though most of these are studies of long oral narratives, there have been attempts at demonstrating the formulaic style in shorter, lyrical, nonheroic, even written, composition: Parry's own suggestions on the Homeric

Hymns, Hesiod, Sappho, etc., followed by others, Robert C. Culley's work on the Psalms (1967), Wang's on the Chinese *Shih Ching* (1971). K. Kailasapathy (1968), in his *Tamil Heroic Poetry,* has shown the relevance of formulaic studies, and studies of "heroic poetry" in general, to Tamil *puṟam* poems.

The analogies illuminate Tamil poetry and poetics, and put Tamil in a worldwide comparative perspective. Here I shall summarize what we know of the "oral" elements in this poetry and suggest a critique.

The Bards

That classical Tamil poetry is close to an oral base is clear. The poems mention different kinds of bards with their female counterparts, and characteristic instruments (see Kailasapathy 1968:chapter 2 and Hart 1975:chapter 6). They may be classified as in chart 3.

None of the bards described seem to be concerned with writing; even the wise men, *pulavar,* are praised for their unfailing "tongues." The chief meter of the classical poem, *akaval,* is derived from a verb *akavu,* "to utter a sound as a peacock, sing, call, summon." *Akavuṉar, akavalar* or *akavar* are the war bards, are "callers, summoners"; according to a commentator, they recall the memory of the

Chart 3. The Bards

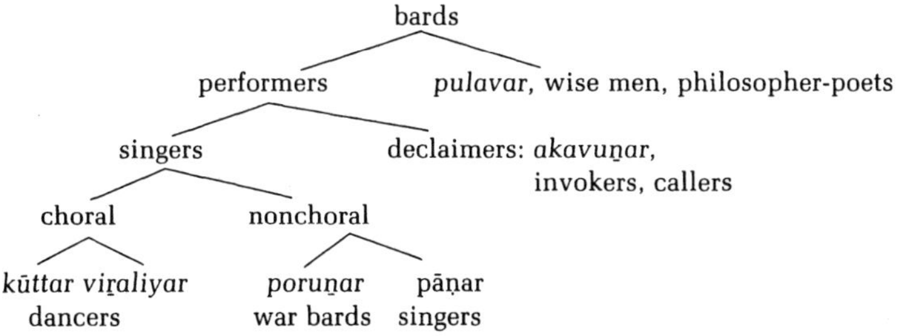

forefathers of the person they are praising. *Akaval* seems to have been a meter suited to reciting more than singing: the *akavuṉar* and the *akavaṉ makaḷir* (women bards) are not assigned any musical instrument (as the *pāṇars* and others are), but a *kōl,* staff or wand.

A commentator says, "the *ōcai,* rhythmic flow peculiar to the meter is to be found among carpenters (at a house-warming ritual?), those hailing the threshing-floor (also field of battle), those prophesying with the aid of paddy and molucca-bean, those waiting and huddled together" (quoted by Kailasapathy 1968:67). The meter's connection with magic, soothsaying, exorcism, and significant rituals like those of house-warming, harvesting, war, and death, as well as with oral chants and spells, seems to be an old one. The common word for language, utterance, both poetic and nonpoetic, was *kēḷvi, kiḷavi,* "that which is heard."

Yet there is no reason to believe that the bards *in* the poems were the poets who composed the poems. In the poems, a distinction is made between the *pulavar,* "wise men, philosopher-poets" who are clearly named (e.g., Māṅkuṭi Marutaṉ in Puṟanāṉūru 72, quoted on p. 290) and the others, bards, minstrels, dancers, *pāṇar, viṟali,* etc. The latter are always dramatis personae in the poems, or speakers of monologue poems (e.g., *Puṟanāṉūru* 103), but the poems are clearly composed by a *pulavar* with a name or epithet (Auvaiyār, Kapilar, Paraṇar). The name of the meter itself seems to have changed in classical times from *akaval,* "call, summons," to *āciriyam* "the [school-?] master's meter." *Āciriyam* is from *āciriyar* (Skt. *ācārya*), "master, learned man." Further, whatever may be the oral status of the original poems, they were certainly compiled by editors who wrote them down from either their own or others' memories, in the early centuries B.C. or A.D. Certainly the meter and diction of the verse, the creation of traditional formulas and a stock of themes is the work of previous ages (or Caṅkams, Academies, in Tamil mythic terms), which the poets inherited and used. But the authors *of* the poems and the nameless bards *in* the poems clearly are not the same. The poems are not the result of rapid composition like oral epics, but of subtle care and reworking:

> like a chariot wheel
> made thoughtfully
> over a month
> by a carpenter
> who tosses off eight chariots
> in a day.

Whether they composed them mentally, as blind Milton did, or in writing, is not clear. Yet the authors were close to the stock-in-trade of bards and minstrels who were often their subjects and who were very much alive all around them. The poems are witnesses to a transition.

Formulas and Other "Elements of Production"

A formula, for Parry (1971:13), is "a group of words which is regularly employed under the metrical conditions to express a given essential idea." Rapid oral composition of many long poems over a stretch of time in a single strict meter like the Greek hexameter or the Tamil *akaval* requires a varied but finite stock of metrically fitting phrases. The most common of them is the *epithet + noun* for heroes, objects, animals, birds, etc. The well-known Homeric examples are "rosy-fingered dawn," "winged words"; every chief character in Homer has a fixed epithet.[10]

There is no reason, however, to believe as Parry did, that "formulaic" and "traditional" necessarily meant "oral," only most probably so. "Writers" coexist with "oral traditions." In transitional periods, writing is used by literate poets to compose new work, to record for others, for posterity, or for later oral recitation; the standards and techniques may still be oral, formulaic. In a famous opening passage, Kumāravyāsa, the fifteenth-century author of the Kannada *Mahābhārata,* with at least six centuries of "written" tradition behind him, wrote that his "excellences" *(aggaḷike)* were those of "not erasing a word after putting it down," "of not letting the sound of the stylus ever cease"—just as oral poets cannot erase a word or allow a break in their flow of words. His long epic, clearly meant and used (to this day) for public recitation was composed in writing. Yet it is very close tc an oral tradition, mostly written in a single meter, and full of the formulas, enjambments, type-scenes characteristic of oral narratives. Similar observations can be made of Kamba<u>n</u>'s twelfth-century Tamil *Rāmāyaṇa* or Tuḷasi's Hindi *Rāmacaritamānasa.* They wrote in the ambience of living oral traditions which are alive to this day. The interplay between written and oral composition in India is just beginning to be studied.[11] Classical Tamil verse is a good place to study it.

Now, the Tamil "elements of production" could be arranged briefly and conveniently at each level, in an ascending order of larger and larger size-units, as the *Tolkāppiyam* does. Chart 4 gives some examples.

The meter and formulas are matched closely. The formulaic elements, at the level of the word, mediate between metrical needs and theme choices, so that every thematic element has ready-made traditional words and word groups which fit different lengths of the meter.

Traditional formulas or formulaic phrases come in different sizes. So they may fit one- or two-syllable units[12] (called *nēr* or *nirai,* and these words are themselves examples of the units) or a foot (combination of the above

Chart 4. Tamil Elements of Production

SOUND: *Meter* *(ceyyuḷ)*	WORD: *Formulaic elements* *(coṟṟoṭar)*	DISCOURSE: *Ideas* *(poruḷ)*
units of meter, "feet," "syllabic patterns," "movement"	standard epithet	motifs
aṭi, line	epithet and noun to fit one or more feet in a line	themes, "type-scenes," situations *(tuṟai)*
yāppu, rhythm, "weave of verse," longer than a line	longer formulas	genres *(tiṇai)* of love poetry and heroic poetry

units), two feet, a whole line, or units running over more than one line. For instance, a one-syllable word, *val*, "strong" may be used with bows *(valvil)*, lances *(valvēl)*, etc.; *valvēl*, "strong lance" may be used as a unit with names like Cāttaṉ, Malaiyaṉ, Pāṇaṉ, all giving half-lines. One may substitute *pal*, "many," for *val*, "strong," and *vāḷ*, "sword," for *vēl*, "lance," without changing metrical values, and we get more interchangeable combinations; when these are applied to heroes' names like Vaḷavaṉ, Pāṇaṉ, Vēntaṉ, Kuṭṭuvaṉ, Āṇṭiraṉ, Evvi, Piṭṭaṉ, we get a wider range of substitution patterns, within different lengths and parts of the metrical frame. Thus we have a paradigmatic system, with a set of interchangeable members in each "slot":

Adjective	*Noun*	*Generic or Proper Name*
strong	chariot sword lance	Evvi Piṭṭaṉ Aṇṇal

Similarly, we can have formulas for cities: "Uṟantai of trusted might"; plants and flowers: "strong-stemmed kino"; birds: "red-eared eagle"; animals both wild and domesticated: "elephant well trained in war"; sky, cloud, waterfall, sun, moon, villages, streets, musical instruments: "husky-voiced drum," "black-handled small harp," and so on, until we have an extensive lexicon of useful vocabulary (or "formulary") of various metrical lengths capable of combining with other such formulaic elements. Furthermore, the same adjective can go with many nouns to make compound epithets that may also qualify many nouns, and the whole phrase can be used as a unit, or declined and placed with other constituents of a sentence, or inflected. Thus *peruṅkal nāṭaṉ* "the chieftain of the lofty hills" can be subject, object, vocative, part of a genitive phrase, etc., can occur as the first half or last half of a line. Similarly there are recurring verb phrases, like "returning to the old home," and phrases that cover three feet of a line, or all four feet, like "where is he gone, my lord and stay?" "the potter in the wide-placed old village"—describing men, objects, or actions ("seeking the dark wide and cool sea"). By adding and interlocking these set phrases, the formulaic elements may cover more than one line—usually in the longer poem, as in *Pattuppāṭṭu* and *Patiṟṟuppattu*. Other such longer units are favorite opening and ending formulas; forms of address and blessing; and refrains "I laugh whenever I think of it"). Interested readers will find references and hundreds of examples for Tamil in Kailasapathy (1968:134–86), and for other languages in Parry (1971), Lord (1960), Bowra (1952), and others. As Kailasapathy (1968:182) rightly says, "the evidence of the early Tamil poems and particularly the *Tolkāppiyam* is astonishingly close to the findings of modern researchers of oral poetry."

We must remember that the formulaic elements are not static counters even in oral verse-making. For instance, a formula like "Where is he gone, my lord and stay?" occurs in the anthologies four times, in different contexts and genres: twice in elegies (e.g., p. 170) lamenting the death of a king and of a nameless hero, and in love poems where the woman is pining for her lover who is far away; in the elegies, the question is rhetorical for the hero is dead, whereas in the love poem the question is a literal one, wondering where he is now. Yet like words in the first language, the formulaic elements in the bardic second language are not fixed in meaning, but quite sensitive to usage and context, and must be attended to, as one would in reading or re-reading any other poem.

Many changes are rung by skillful bards on the basic pattern. Analogical formation keeps close to the metrical and grammatical patterns, but rings changes not only on single words but often on the entire verse, the tone, the subject:

> "The ships come with gold and return with pepper."
>
> "The waves come with shrimps and recede with garlands."

When such changes are rung, the strict meaning of the term "formula" loses its rigor. The members no longer form a class, but are more like a family (in Wittgenstein's sense), representing various degrees of resemblance and connection. Actually, the second language of artifice begins to work more and more like a natural first language. The idea behind each family of forms, behind the so-called variants, is not a clear norm, one source formula, but a gestalt, an intuitive preverbal semantic form, a *sphoṭa,* as Sanskrit semiologists would say (Nagler 1974:13–15).

Situations and Frames

As metrical constraints organize sounds and rhythms into verse, formulaic elements select and organize the word-stock of the language toward the diction of verse. Similarly, in the realm of meanings, a stock of themes, leitmotivs, motifs, incidents, type-scenes (battle scenes, trysts, etc.)

organizes and stylizes topics and contexts for poetry. Seventy-eight such "situations" *(tuṟai)* are listed for the *puṟam* poems (for details, see Kailasapathy 1968:185 ff.). The groupings in this book use some of them, e.g., heroic mothers, praise of chieftains, elegies. In love poems, one may cite the various contexts in which a girl friend might speak.

The colophons and commentators, as we have seen, assume for each poem a heading, a situation, a frame, a fictive world of speakers, hearers (and overhearers), times and places. These frames add subtleties and dramatic ironies. The wedding poem quoted earlier carries the colophon, "What he said, after a quarrel, remembering their wedding night." Without the heading, the poem is a fine description of a man remembering his wedding night and his bride's shyness. With the heading, it is a *marutam* poem, a poem of infidelity: he returns home early one morning after a night with his concubine and finds the door shut in his face. Sitting outside his house, he remembers his wedding night and the shyness of his new bride (now an angry wife). In such poems, the *marutam* situation of "door-shutting" frames the memory of love and marriage *(kuṟiñci* and *mullai).* The frame gives it a piquancy and humor, allows us and the speaker to look at an experience in two ways at once. Landscape genres, situations, indications of speakers and listeners—all of them provide such turns and ironies.

The following poem, the very first in *Kuṟuntokai,* uses frame within frame thrice over:

What Her Girl Friend Said
to him, refusing his gift of red flowers

Red is the battlefield
as he crushes
the demons,
red his arrow shafts,

red the tusks
of his elephants:

this is the hill
of the Red One
with the whirling anklets,

the hill of red glory lilies,
flowers of blood.

Tipputtōḷār
Kuṟuntokai 1

On the face of it, the description could be from a war poem, in praise of a chieftain. The reference to demons and the Red One (Cēyōṉ or Murukaṉ) enlists the war imagery to praise a god of war, the god of the hills, which makes it a religious poem. The title of the poem, "What her girl friend said to him, refusing his gift of red flowers," adds a third frame. The girl friend is describing a god's plenty of red flowers on the Red One's hills, not at all to praise the god but to reject the suitor's gift of red flowers, a love token. If she or her friend accepted them, that would be tantamount to accepting his tryst. It is a *kuṟiñci* poem set in the hills; the girl friend is teasingly delaying love's consummation. Thus a war poem is set inside a religious one, which in turn is used to make a love poem. Three major genres are here, frame within frame.

In early classical poetry, such religious allusions in the love poems invariably have an erotic agenda; they are part of the love game. In some war poems, a hero is compared to a god who is explicitly praised; the god's praise becomes part of a tribute to the hero. In postclassical poetry, the converse pattern prevails: love and war motifs serve the ends of religious poetry. The motifs, the signifiers, come from the same stock; they do not change in form, but in significance. The frames change the poems.

A bard acquires these resources from memorizing past poems, often apprenticing himself to a senior bard, singing with or behind him in public performances; he not only inherits them; he shares them with other bards of his time. As he grows and matures, he moves from imitating them to adapting them to his own use (the parallels with native Indian music, dance, and architecture are irresistible).

As in many other early traditions—whether Greek, Sanskrit, Celtic, or Chinese—poetry, science, and magic meet in a bard. Bards and poets are the custodians of the highest knowledge of the age—"whether of the past, in the form of history and genealogy; of the hidden present, in the form commonly of scientific information; and of the future, in the form of prophetic utterance in the narrower sense" (Chadwick 1942:14). As we have seen, the *Tolkāppiyam*, like other bardic grammars, includes in its third book a cosmology, a taxonomic classification of all the elements of an ecosystem, a detailed code of behavior in love and war, a rhetoric which deals with meters, genres, themes, and wordlists. A Tamil classical poet inherits this repertoire and is trained in it; he does not think about tradition, he thinks with it, within it. Tradition, in this precise sense, provides him his material, his medium, his model, his universe of signifiers.

Transpositions

Though language consists of signs made of signifiers and signifieds, such signs are continually transformed. They become signifiers in a secondary system of connotations (Barthes 1967:89). The signs of this secondary system become in turn the signifiers of expressive systems like mythology; poetry weaves into its language all the cultural significances of words and things, their mythic and ritual uses, and "returns" them to ordinary language, however indirectly, making a rich many-layered set of signifiers—renewing the "language of the tribe." At its simplest, take *mayil,* the word for a peacock in Tamil, the first language of Tamil culture. *Mayil* signifies, in usage and connotation, "beauty," "vanity," etc.; in mythology, Lord Murukaṉ's vehicle; and in classical poetry, lovers' union, femininity, etc. The interested reader may follow peacocks and their various uses (or elephants, or herons) throughout the poems. In the following poem, a peacock is paired with a bull elephant, its counterpart in religious poems (as a vehicle for Murukaṉ), in war (strength, majesty), and in love poems (a beast of the hills, leader of herds, representing the lover's virility, his wildness):

What Her Girl Friend Said
to him

Sir,
  not that we did not hear the noise
  you made trying to open the bolted doors,
  a robust bull elephant
  stirring in the night
  of everyone's sleep;
we did. But as we fluttered inside
like a peacock in the net,
crest broken, tail feathers flying,

our good mother held us close
in her innocence
thinking to quell our fears.

Kaṇṇaṉ
Kuṟuntokai 244

So no good bard is only a reciter, nor does his art simply reproduce a past poem. He uses the whole tradition as his instrument, a keyboard, a language of possibilities. The signifiers may remain the same, but what is signified continually changes, in Tamil (and early Indian) poetry.

No two poems of these Eight Anthologies are alike, though the art language is the same. Every instance resonates in counterpoint with all the other uses of the whole tradition of themes, pictures, formulas. The individual poem as a whole is not predictable, in either its inner form or its nuance—though its parts are given. Enumerating its components (formulas, etc.) is only to enumerate an "elements list"; it only describes the materials and the medium of the particular poem—hardly describes, analyzes, or evaluates the poem. (It is unfortunate that in Kailasapathy's excellent work on *Tamil Heroic Poetry*, he does not look at a single poem *as a poem* in detail.) The poem remains to be read, as any other poem, oral or written; the language of the past becomes present in it. The old commentators do not merely note the similarities of themes and phrases shared across poems; they attend to the grammatical, rhetorical, and poetic individuality of each poem. I have tried to follow their example. The poems in this book and the few analyses of single poems that appear here in this afterword, I hope, demonstrate that there is another code, the poetic, which organizes the formulaic and all other traditional codes that the poet inherits and habitually composes with. Individual poems are created out of all the given "elements of production," and all the language of past poems.

What She Said

Only the thief was there, no one else.
And if he should lie, what can I do?

There was only
a thin-legged heron

standing on legs yellow as millet stems
and looking
for lampreys
in the running water
when he took me.

Kapilar
Kuṟuntokai 25

Some features of this poem do occur elsewhere once or twice in the anthologies: the word "thief" applied to the lover, the millet-stem legs of the heron, looking for fish in the water while they are secretly making love. Yet checking through the references, we find none of them "formulaic" in the sense described earlier. Furthermore, as Naccinārkkiṉiyar's old commentary points out, the predatory nature of the heron is what is in focus. The bird looking for fish in the running waters is like the lover taking his woman. From another point of view, the unseeing, uncaring bird also represents the world. The commentator also notes the singular number of the heron: the loneliness of the place, the singular heron who is not attending to anything but his own prey, the lack of witnesses, are part of the suggestion. And the woman remembers the heron vividly because it crystallizes her fears regarding her lover's possible treachery. Though the poem is firmly set in *kuṟiñci* (lovers' union, the millet stems), the water and the heron seem subtly to suggest *neytal* (anxious waiting), and the mood is close to *marutam* (infidelity) or fear of it. Thus, the vivid moment of love-making (with which the poem climaxes) and the focused image of the predatory heron, representing that moment, that stays in the woman's mind, contain past experience, present doubts, and future fears; three different landscapes are suggested. The predicate with the heron as the subject, *uṇṭu*, "is, was, will be" depending on the context, is apt in its generality (as Nacciṉārkkiṉiyar says). I need not point out the way the exterior landscape becomes also an interior one in the course of the poem. Though many of the elements, like the words of a language, are given, the poem is created anew. What is not given by the tradition of conventions, and comes into being with this poem by this poet, is the inner form, the pattern of allusion, of metaphor, poetic design, grammatical subtlety, the flow of images, sensuous evocation, psychological insight.

The poem is thus a mosaic of given forms, and a dance of meanings as well.

"Originality"

The notion of originality is itself a recent convention. "Copyright" and "plagiarism" are its legal complements. Post-Romantic notions (in India as well as elsewhere) of "originality," imply that (a) tradition and convention are impediments to creativity, and that (b) originality consists in "originating" both the total form of the poem and each element in it. This position, of course, leads one to think of an "individual talent" as opposed to "tradition," vying Oedipally with past masters; every author is a belated arrival who has to prove himself new—and subject to the "anxiety of influence" that Harold Bloom (1973) has devoted himself to describing. An old Sanskrit epigram describes the dilemma of Bloom's writer, Johnny-come-lately: "If you have not read the ancients, how can you write? If you have read the ancients, *why* do you write?" But the Tamil poets do not seem to be anxious. They are continuous with their past. Tradition is their language for poetry, which they share with their masters, their peers, and their immediate audience—they both learn and modify it. When

T. S. Eliot (1950:5) speaks of the individual poem altering ever so slightly the whole traditional order, he was describing the ancient classical poets more accurately than he was describing most modern writers of Europe—every realized poem changes somewhat our idea of poetry itself, yet fulfills a potential in the tradition. But for a modern poet like Eliot, tradition is made retrospectively by the individual poet; hence, his tradition is not the same as Yeats's, or Pound's, though all three were contemporaries and advocates of what each called Tradition. In contrast, individual Tamil poets inherit, share, and are made by the tradition. As the creatures and creators of their tradition the Caṅkam poems make "infinite use of finite means," generating novelty without defying tradition or quarreling with the given means.

This Indian Oedipus does not slay his father, but obeys and fulfills him, often sacrificing his potency for his elders (as Bhīṣma did in the epic). At his best, he becomes himself (and is acclaimed as a hero) by first surrendering to them. These poets did not feel, as (Romantic) Wordsworth or some modern Indian poets do, that "every genius has to create the taste by which he is to be read." Creativity appears as the full present use of a given language. The whole actualized poem is still new, not predictable.

Neither should it be imagined that there were no standards among the poets, just because they all used the same poetic language. The very presence of anthologies of good poems carefully selected out of a possible great number is contrary to such a notion. Individual poets were known for their masterly work in one or another genre or landscape. A poet like Kapilar was so renowned for his many *kuṟiñci* poems that even late poems of that genre (in *Kalittokai*, 6th century?) were assigned to him. Names like Pālaipāṭiya Peruṅkatuṅkō means "Peruṅkaṭuṅkō who sang *pālai* songs."

I noted earlier how certain others were remembered and named for their resonant phrases, e.g., Cempulappeyaṉīrār, "the poet of the red earth and pouring rain."

Values

Much has been written on the values, the religion, the politics, the social and economic life of the early Tamils, drawing mostly on the references in the poems. The interested reader may turn to works like Nilakanta Sastry (1966) or Subramanian (1966). Kailasapathy (1968) and Hart (1975) are particularly interested in the ethos and the value system. Here I shall confine my remarks only to the early classical poems and suggest certain striking characteristics of the world they project.

The classical Tamil poems embody values, but do not speculate or philosophize about them. They do not elaborate a mythology. In a sense, the poems are unified by the world-picture which functions like a mythology.

In it, nature and culture are not opposed but consubstantial; together they make meanings possible, each containing the other in paradoxes of metonymy. And the metonymy generates metaphors—the natural scene with its many orders is *like* the human scene because the two belong together. A landscape *(tiṇai)*, in the Tamil definition, is both a place and a mood; to speak of one is to evoke the other. Contemplating this kind of view, one sees that the nature/culture opposition is itself a culture-bound notion. For cultures like the classical Tamil, "nature-culture," a hyphenated continuum, seems to make better sense. One might go further and say that each of these ways of looking at "nature and culture" is accompanied by different kinds of poetics and favorite figures (as I suggested earlier in passing; see, for further suggestions, Ramanujan 1970a).

To these must be added the situations *(tuṟai)*, the characters of *akam* and *puṟam* poems, their decorum, and their passion.

All these together express an aesthetic, an ethos, and a world view consonant with one another. We have spoken so far only of the first and the last. In this section, I shall speak of the middle term, "ethos."

The characteristic genius of this poetry is in its lack of metaphysical abstraction; even its most complex thinking is done in terms of physical detail. In all 2,381 poems, hardly 13 (all in *Puṟanāṉūṟu;* see "Lessons," pp. 155 ff.), are didactic—in fact, these strike one as rather specially stoic and Jain in tone. Even the cosmology does not dwell on the first elements, origins, or the creator. Indeed no creator god is envisaged here, nor is Nature conceived as a whole or as a creative spirit. The gods and demons are part of the human and natural scene, immanent, worshiped or feared in certain places, trees, water, and stone (see "His Places," p. 215). Though, as George Hart (1975) has eloquently shown, the sacred is pervasive, enforced by taboo and danger, present in woman's breast and royal drum, propitiated by dance and offering, I think it is still not the explicit concern of this early poetry, only of the later *Paripāṭal* and the *Guide to Lord Murukaṉ* (see Book 4)—where Sanskritic myths and notions of god seem to have met and married the local Tamil ideas of *akam* and *puṟam*. Here we see a god treated as a Tamil king with all his insignia—whereas elsewhere, in Sanskrit and in later Tamil, kings are representatives and emblems of the gods. Tamil words like *kō* and *iṟai* seem to have meant "king" first and "god" later; they were protectors and destroyers; *kōyil* meant both "palace" and "temple." It is not surprising that both Māyōṉ or Tirumāl the Dark One, and Murukaṉ or Cēyōṉ the Red One, seem to be typical early Tamil gods, and they were gods of love as well as war. The former is assimilated to Viṣṇu/Kṛṣṇa in *bhakti* poetry, as the latter to Skanda, enlisting Sanskritic mythologies, leading to complex developments. I refer the reader to the many studies of these figures and of the immensely important Śiva (e.g., Clothey 1978, Zvelebil 1977, Shulman 1980, Nilakanta Sastry 1966, for South India).

Though the many lives *(maṟumai)* of a person or the *ūḻ* (past deeds?) are mentioned, they seem only hyperbolic or metaphoric. The reward of the hero who dies in battle is often an afterworld of pleasure, an elysium, a heaven of heroes.

Not even the rousing abstraction of a whole nation or a kingdom is the subject of song—though a Tamil territory, a Tamiḻakam is mentioned. Only the individual king or hero, his battles, his bounty, his justice, and his life, are poetic subjects. Loyalty is loyalty to a master, not to an idea or a community. Even in war, the hero is known for his valor and prowess rather than for any kind of large-scale military organization or strategy. Elegies like *Puṟanāṉūru* 239 (p. 171) are telling portraits of the hero. Neither the romance of an ideal nor patriotism toward a country makes this poetry heroic; what makes it heroic is the stirring presence of particular men and women—three warring kings each with his own emblematic flowers, the many chieftains with their sacred drums and guardian trees, the many more unknown warriors, their wives, widows, and mothers, sung by the bards in panegyric and elegy. Furthermore,

> Not rice,
> not water,
> only the king
> is the life-breath
> of a kingdom.
>
> And it is the duty

of a king
with his army of spears
to know
he's the life
of the wide, blossoming kingdom.

Mōcikīraṉār (or Mātimātirattaṉār)
Puṟanāṉuṟu 186

When he forgets he is "the life," and does wrong, he brings death, famine, and disorder to his country, because he is one with it, as the lovers are one with their landscapes. It is significant that he is described as "a king with his army of spears." The entire society in the *puṟam* poems is geared to the values of war, to fashioning a warrior "like a chariot wheel":

To bring forth and rear a son is my duty.
To make him noble is the father's.
To make spears for him is the blacksmith's.
To show him good ways is the king's.

And to bear
a bright sword and do battle,
to butcher enemy elephants,
and come back:

that is the young man's duty.

Poṉmuṭiyār
Puṟanāṉūṟu 312

Honor *(pukaḻ)*, fame, a good name *(peyar)* in life or in death, in legend and bardic poetry, are what a man seeks; a sense of shame *(nāṇ)* controls that seeking, from within. The woman values and guards above all her "sexual honor" or chastity *(kaṟpu)* and her virtue and modesty *(nalaṉ)*. As the man fears disgrace, cowardice, turning his back on the enemy, she constantly fears betrayal and abandonment by her man. There is no *femme fatale*, no *belle dame sans merci*, in these poems.

These values are enforced by *paḻi* or blame in public, often blame in the mouths of poets. In the *akam* poem, the woman fears *alar*, neighbors' gossip, the public use of her name. Thus the *akam/puṟam* or interior/exterior distinction also organizes the positive and negative values:

Interior	*Exterior*	*"Name"*
virtue, *nalaṉ*	honor, *pukaḻ*	praise, poetry, *kēḷvi*
shame, *nāṇ*	blame, *paḻi*	gossip, *alar*

When a man dies in battle, he should have no wounds in his back—a mother is enraged by the rumor that her son died with his back to the enemy (p. 182). Even when a man-child dies in infancy, he is quartered, before his funeral rites, as if in battle (p. 120).

It is the business of the bards to keep honor alive. The bards, wandering "tribal encyclopedias," custodians and transmitters of past history, present science, and prophetic knowledge, carry the good name of good men into the future as well as to others, and present the hero to himself.

In *Puṟanāṉūṟu* 72, the young king, Neṭuñceḻiyaṉ, pained by the insults of enemy kings, cries out:

> If I do not scatter them
> in battle
> and capture them,
> drums and all,
> . . .
> may [my people]
> call their king heartless,
> my scepter be cursed
> by their tears and blame!
> . . .
> May the poets
> led by Māṅkuṭi Marutaṉ,

that poet of noble speech,
may the poets
longstanding as the world
shun
and leave unsung
the borders of my land!

The poets were the articulate bearers of honor and blame, and so they had the power to counsel, to sneer and curse, and to make peace and to point to the vanity of human, even royal, wishes (see p. 121). They were the censors and mirrors, the memories and superegos of the heroic milieu. As friends of kings, they often died with them, as bards did in the case of Kōpperuñcōḻaṉ—who when his sons rose in arms against him and disgraced his lineage, starved himself to death, sitting facing north with his entire court. The bards also kept up the morale of the warriors by singing their past ancestors in genealogies, the gore and smoke of present battle, and of the loot soldiers would share if they survived, and of the great posthumous honor if they did not. The generic names for the bards clearly indicate their connections with war: *akavuṉar,* "callers, invokers," *viṟali,* from *viṟal* "war frenzy," and *poruṉar* "war bards"; the last were also called *porā poruṉar* "the unwarring warriors": they obviously accompanied the army to battle. A legendary warrior is said to have bequeathed his skin to be made into the war drum of his tribe, to inspire later warriors every time it was sounded. The Tamil bards drummed on such drums of war.

The bards and heroes, munificent patrons and gifted suppliants, together made the world of the Noble Ones, *cāṉṟōr,* an important value-loaded word in this aristocratic culture. Many poems celebrate the patron's "giving" *(ītal, īkai),* his bounty, the rivers of wine and the mounds of meat (e.g., p. 146).

Not only food and drink, but gold, elephants, and chariots are given as gifts. Such often unconditional sharing is a much-prized virtue—later, religious poems conceive of god's grace *(aruḷ)* in similar terms. The relations of bard and patron in these early poems parallel those of brahman and king later, and of devotee and god. Gift giving which begins as exchange, as circulation of wealth, goes beyond it to celebration, excess, display, overflow in the potlatch of the chieftains, and in the greater potlatch of god's grace and bounty, till it seems that the Chieftain of Chieftains cannot do without it. As the saint-poet Nammāḻvār (eighth century?) says, using *puṟam* formulas to reject the human patrons to whom they were originally addressed, transvaluing *puṟam* values (Ramanujan 1981):

> My lord of a thousand names
>   gives and gives
>
> the fame of his giving
>   crosses all boundaries
>
> I cannot praise anyone else
>   cannot say to some paltry thing
>   of this world:
>
>   "Your hand is bounteous as the rain,
>   your shoulders are strong as the mountains"
>
> I cannot tell such barefaced lies

Sometimes in the *akam* poems, the poet, through his personae, makes fun of his poetic conventions; in the *puṟam* poems the poet cocks a snook at other poets' sycophantic ravings, and laughs gently at the importance of chieftains:

> Pāri! Pāri! they cry,
> these poets
> with their good red tongues,
> praising one man
> in many ways:

yet it's not only Pāri,

the rains too
keep the world
going
in these parts.

The cycles about chieftains like Pāri and Āy (pp. 137 ff.) record the passing of a world of petty chiefdoms; they were besieged and devoured by kings with great armies. One of the most moving of these cycles is about Pāri at the peak of his power and in his fall, about his bravery, his bravado against the Big Three voiced by his poet-friend Kapilar, in poems like *Puṟanāṉūṟu* 109 (p. 142):

. . .
He will not give in
to the sword.

But I know a way
to take it:

pick carefully
your lute-strings, string little lutes,
and with your dancing women
with dense fragrant hair
behind you,
go singing and dancing
to Pāri,

and he'll give you
both hill and country.

A number of grim poems at the core of the *Puṟanāṉūṟu* are about unknown warriors, their fall, their waiting sons, their wives ready to bury themselves alive in their husbands' burial urns, and mothers who rejoice in their sons' heroic death. These passages are red with heroic gore:

. . .
blood glows,
like the sky before nightfall,

in the red center
of the battlefield.

Demons dance there.

And your kingdom
is an unfailing harvest
of victorious wars.

Patiṟṟuppattu 35

Note the reference to harvest; war was for plunder, sharing, and survival. Harvest also suggests the returning cycles of generations, and brings fertility and death together (Hart 1975:40).

One sees a certain epic quality in the *puṟam* anthologies: in the cycles of poems on Pāri's great career, his legendary extravagant gesture of leaving his chariot for a poor creeper to train itself on, his self-sufficient hill later ravaged by enemies, his two daughters left in the care of his poet-friend Kapilar, who sees past glory and present wreckage; or in the episodes (not included in this book) of Kōpperuñcōḻaṉ fasting unto death, facing north, surrounded by henchmen, and sending for his poet-friend—who arrives from his faraway home several days late, in time only to mourn his great friend's ruin; or the cycle of poems about the unknown warriors. In these one feels the power and pathos of the *puṟam* poems, so different in tone and significance from the poignant, humane *akam*, yet composed often by the same poets. Kailasapathy (1968:27) and others feel that many *puṟam* poems must have been fragments of a lost epic. But the single poems are too well-formed and artistically climaxed to be fragments. Rather, these cycles, characters, episodes, and the whole second language of heroic poetry that developed over centuries seem to have waited for a Homer-like epic poet to master and weld them into one great epic action—for a Tamil Homer who never arrived.

During the fourth century, the political circumstances changed; the early dynasties had weakened, yielding to confusion, "a dark age of the Kalabhras" about which we know little. Then came the Pallavas (c. A.D. 500–900), and with them Tamil had to come to terms with courtly Sanskrit and everything it represented. This creative meeting led to a new religious consciousness called bhakti, new uses for *akam* and *puṟam* motifs in religious thinking and in making poems about gods. The Tamil sense of the sacred, immanent in particular things and places, led soon to the building of temples. Now a god was the king, and the wandering saints were His bards, the temple was His palace (*kōyil*). From the sixth century on, the country was swept by the Nāyaṉmārs and the Āḻvārs, devotees of Śiva and Viṣṇu. Gods and poet-saints had replaced the Noble Ones, the heroes and their bards.

So when Kampaṉ, an epic poet of genius, actually arrived (c. twelfth century?) he chose for his hero the divine Rāma, bypassing the earlier heroic themes and cycles, but assimilating the older poetic language to entirely new uses. Under the sway of bhakti (Nammāḻvār is his supposed master), Kampaṉ could not have directly sung a human hero. No Hindu *Rāmāyaṇa* composed after the tenth century escapes the pervasive ambience of bhakti; the very telling of the Rāma story becomes an act of devotion to Rāma.

The Afterlife of Akam and *Puṟam*

Caṅkam poetry changes thus from early to late classical forms, toward explicitly religious poems. As sheer poetry, it was not to be surpassed by any later achievement; passion and precision, power and courtesy, range and economy, met here as they have rarely met in any body of Indian lyric poetry. Furthermore, these poems, 2,000 or so in number, besides carrying a great classical culture, set the themes and forms, and standardized the language for later literature, even when for centuries the old poems were eclipsed by religious preoccupations, and were not studied even by pundits.

The early classical conceptions of *akam* and *puṟam* do not die. They find vigorous new lives in every major Tamil text until the twelfth century, and even beyond: in the Love Section of the *Kuṟaḷ*, the fourth-century book of aphorisms that for many contains the quintessence of Tamil wisdom; in the songs and structure of the Anklet Story (*Cilappatikāram*, c. fifth century?); and even in its so-called twin, the unique Buddhist work, *Maṇimēkalai;* in the moving and popular hymns of the Śaiva and Vaiṣṇava saint-poets, and in Kampaṉ himself. All these texts, all except the Buddhist epic, are widely read, recited, and used in temples, festivals, and political platforms today.

As we have seen, the very conception of god and king in South India has its roots in classical poems. Even contemporary Tamil temple myths, rituals, and other religious expressions cannot be fairly understood without them. Furthermore, *akam* and *puṟam* concepts may prove to be still relevant to the study of current folklore and modern Tamil fiction.

Translating a Tamil Poem

Many of the above considerations have gone into the making of these translations—into the many, small, stitch-by-stitch decisions that any translation involves. If one is interested only in the poems, as a reader might very well be, the afterword might be seen as a needless display of the back of the embroidery.

Though only poems can translate poems, a translator is "an artist on oath." He has a double allegiance, indeed, several double allegiances. All too familiar with the rigors and pleasures of reading a text and those of making another, caught between the need to express himself and the need to represent another, moving between the two halves of one brain, he has to use both to get close to "the originals." He has to let poetry win without allowing scholarship to lose. Then his very compromises may begin to express a certain fidelity, and may suggest what he cannot convey. Crossing languages, one ancient or foreign, another current and familiar, searching in one language for forms and tones that will mimic and relive those of another, he may fashion now and then a third that will look like the one and speak like (or for) the other. Yet, more often than not, his task, like Marvell's love, is "begotten by despair upon impossibility."

In translating these poems, I have tried to attend always to the minute particulars of individual poems, the words, the syntax, and through them the world in the words. But I have been haunted by St.-John Perse's ambiguous story of the Mongolian conqueror (1966:40),

> taker of a bird in its nest, and of the nest in its tree, who brought back with bird and nest and song the whole natal tree itself, torn from its place with its multitude of roots, its ball of earth and its border of soil, a remnant of home territory evoking a field, a province, a country, and an empire. . . .

NOTES

Notes to the Translator's Note

1. Tamil, Kannada, Malayalam, and Telugu are the four major Dravidian languages of south India. They are spoken, approximately by 50, 31, 30, and 59 millions in Tamilnadu, Karnataka, Kerala, and Andhra Pradesh states respectively. At least 17 other nonliterary Dravidian languages are scattered all over central, eastern, and western India, the farthest-flung being Brahui, a Dravidian speech-island in today's Pakistan, surrounded by Indo-Aryan and Indo-Iranian languages of the Northwest.

2. The Eight Anthologies and their contents, excluding opening invocations that were added later, were the following:

Akam Anthologies

Kuṟuntokai, "Anthology of Short Poems," 401 love poems, 4–8 lines each, with one 9-line poem; 203 poets.
Naṟṟiṇai, "The Excellent Genres," 399 love poems, 9–12 lines each; 187 poets.
Akanāṉūṟu, "400 love poems," 13–37 lines each; 158 poets.
Aiṅkuṟunūṟu, "500 Short Love Poems" (two missing), each hundred dealing with one of the five conventional phases of love and apparently written by a different poet.
Kalittokai, "Anthology of Kali poems," 150 love poems in a meter called *kali*; 5 poets.

Puṟam Anthologies

Puṟanāṉūṟu, "400 Puṟam Poems" (two missing, 43 with lines missing), 4–40 lines; 157 poets.
Patiṟṟuppattu, the "Ten Tens," 80 poems on kings (with the first ten and the tenth ten missing); 8–57 lines; 8 poets.
Paripāṭal, 24 extant poems and a few fragments in a meter called *paripāṭal*; contains 15 religious poems; 32–140 lines; 13 poets.

Kalittokai and *Paripāṭal* appear to be the latest of the eight anthologies; *Kuṟuntokai* and *Puṟanāṉūṟu* contain probably the earliest compositions.

Pattuppāṭṭu, the Ten Long Poems, contains the following:

Akam

Kuṟiñcippāṭṭu, "A Poem of *Kuṟiñci*" (mountain landscape and lovers' union); 261 lines, by Kapilar.

Puṟam

Porunarāṟṟuppaṭai, "A Guide Poem (*āṟṟuppaṭai*) For Bards Of War"; 248 lines, by Muṭattāmakkaṇṇiyār.

Ciṟupāṇāṟṟuppaṭai, "A Short Guide Poem for Bards With Lutes"; 269 lines, by Naṟṟattaṉār.

Perumpāṇāṟṟuppaṭai, "A Long Guide Poem for Bards with Lutes"; 500 lines, by Uruttiraṅkaṇṇaṉār.

Maturaikkāñci, "Advice [Given in] the City of Maturai"; 782 lines, by Māṅkuṭi Marutaṉār.

Malaipaṭukaṭām, "Echoes on the Mountain"; 583 lines, by Peruṅkuṉṟūr Peruṅkaucikaṉār.

Mixed Genres

Paṭṭiṉappālai, "A *Pālai* (separation) Poem On The City"; 301 lines, by Uruttiraṅkaṇṇaṉār.

Mullaippāṭṭu, "*Mullai* Poem" (jasmine country and the theme of a woman patiently waiting for her lover's return); 103 lines, by Nappūtaṉār.

Neṭunalvāṭai, "The Good, Long North Wind"; 187 lines, by Nakkīrar.

Tirumurukāṟṟuppaṭai, "A Guide-poem for Lord Murukaṉ"—a devotional poem, with *akam* and *puram* elements; 317 lines, by Nakkīrar.

3. *The Tolkāppiyam:*

The *Tolkāppiyam* is the earliest and most authoritative Tamil grammar, an important work in Indian linguistics, and a text essential to any understanding of classical Tamil poetry and culture. What Pāṇinī's grammar is to Sanskrit, the *Tolkāppiyam* is to Tamil.

Of its three sections, the first two deal with linguistic matters (orthography and phonology; morphology and syntax). The third section, on *poruḷ* or "substance, subject matter, meaning," deals with prosody, rhetoric, poetics, genres, themes, codes of behavior, poetic diction, and cultural semantics. Like many other Indian expository texts, this work is presented as a series of *cūttirams* (Sanskrit *sūtra*) or brief verse-sayings. The *Tolkāppiyam* has 1,612 *cūttirams*. There are at least seven commentaries, preserved in part or in their entirety; the earliest is Iḷampūraṇar (eleventh–twelfth century), and the most recent is a seventeenth-century anonymous one. There is no clear, complete, reliable translation of the *Tolkāppiyam* in English.

According to legend and the opinion of some scholars, the grammar antedates the *Caṅkam* poems. But the work is not all of one piece: the first two (grammatical) sections appear to be older than the Anthologies, and the third section (directly relevant to the poems) seems to be of a later date.

As an old text says wisely, "No grammar or rhetoric (*ilakkaṇam*), if no [prior] literature (*ilakkiyam*): no sesame oil, if no sesame seed." While this is certainly true of the explicit grammars, Tamil classical poetry assumes and draws on many old implicit cultural traditions: a cosmology, a precise sense of ecosystems, and a pervasive classification of the elements of the culture itself (see the afterword). The poems imply and use an entire "science of the concrete," which the *Tolkāppiyam* codifies and summarizes. Though parts of the grammatical text are later than the poems, the tradition and the world view the *Tolkāppiyam* represents seem much older. In this sense, it is truly "the old composition."

4. See Zvelebil (1973:23–24) for a brief account of the evidence for the dates 100 B.C.–A.D. 250, which comes from various sources: "archeological finds of Roman coins [in the Tamil area]; tallies between Greek traveler-historians and the Tamil texts, especially the 'war' poems; textual reconstructions from cross-references to poets and patron-kings; and lastly from the linguistic properties of the poems."

See also Nilakanta Sastry (1966).

5. Obviously a Jain count, in multiples of 37. The ancient Jains had a passion for numbers.

Notes to the Poems

As the poems, singly and together, will speak directly to the reader, these notes are minimal, mostly confined to glosses and pointers. Where the relevant detail regarding an item (say, a flower) is clear from the context, or where I have no information, no note is included.

p. 5. This poem, and those on pages 16, 17, 21, 29, 67, 70, 75, 184, 189, and 195 are revised versions of translations from *The Interior Landscape* (Ramanujan 1967), now out of print.

For a discussion of this poem and the kuṟiñci landscape, see the afterword, especially chart 1.

p. 9. "Ten on Lovers' Meetings": from the anthology *Aiṅkuṟunūṟu*, "Five Hundred Short Poems," in five sections, each consisting of 100 poems by a single poet, devoted to one of the five landscapes. The 100 poems, in turn, consist of 10 decades. The ten poems of each decade are variations on a theme. Landscapes, situations, often the speakers and phrases ("Bless you . . .") relate the ten to each other. Often there is a progression.

Like Indian music, architecture, and much else in Indian culture, these poems develop a complex mood, a situation, a dwelling place, a mode or raga, by original recombinations, placements, and repetitions of a given set of motifs.

In one sense, all *kuṟiñci* (or *pālai*, etc.) poems are variants of one another—which is my reason for juxtaposing such poems from different anthologies.

Though every one of these ten poems begins with *vāḻi* ("Bless you"), some of my translations drop the phrase or move it.

These poems contain a large number of *kuṟiñci* motifs: parrots, millet crops, jackfruit, hillsmen, kino, elephant, tiger, bamboo, clouds on the hill.

Hill tribes: *kuṟavar* in Tamil (for those who wish to know the special Tamil term).

p. 12. kino: *vēṅkai*, a tree with yellow flowers. Several poems play on the resemblance of the yellow flowers with black stems to the stripes of the tiger. *Vēṅkai* means both kino tree and tiger. Tigers are the natural enemies of the elephants.

Here, and elsewhere, I've chosen to translate Tamil names of flora and fauna into approximate English equivalents, with the help of the *Tamil Lexicon*, the OED, and botanists like Cāmi and Gamble. (See also the index of English, Tamil, and Latin plant names at the end of the book.)

p. 26. Note how a war image (*puṟam* element) is used ironically in an *akam* poem by convention; though *akam* poems are not supposed to mention names as *puṟam* poems do, poets sometimes break the rule, as here, especially in metaphors.

Koṅkar: a warlike tribe of the Koṅku region (today's S-W districts in Tamilnadu); also a common name for the Cēra kings and their armies, rivals of the Pāṇṭiya kings (one of whom is mentioned here). Little else is known about Atikaṉ except this (and one other) poetic reference.

p. 30. Patches of pallor, freckles (*tēmal*), etc. are seen as symptoms of lovesickness.

p. 31. For *neytal* (pronounced *neydal*), see chart 1 in the afterword.

p. 33. laurel: *puṉṉai*, a seaside tree, Alexandrian laurel; described as a tree with "branches black as iron, dark bluish-green waxen leaves, silver white flowers, golden yellow pollen, and its buds shaped like a sparrow's eggs" (Cāmi 1967).

their spirals turning right: the clockwise direction of spirals in oysters, conch shells, etc. is highly valued as auspicious. It is the direction of the sun, the direction of a devotee's circumambulations round a temple, a god, or an elder.

p. 36. Many of the *neytal* motifs cluster together in this poem: seaside, salt pans, blue lily, crab, fishermen, boats, shark, oyster, Koṟkai.

Koṟkai: ancient seaport on the southeast coast, known for its pearl fishery.

p. 39. Four poems chosen out of ten on the tigerclaw tree (*ñāḻal*, or *pulinakakkoṉṟai*). The flowers look like tiger claws.

p. 43. In these six (chosen out of ten), the experienced concubines tease their man about his new girl friend (wife?) who is very young, even sexually immature. I have followed the original in placing these poems in *neytal*, though the theme is *marutam*.

The relations between the concubine and the wife of the man are subtle, the attitudes complex, in these poems. See also pp. 94, 102, 103.

p. 51. For *pālai*, see chart 1 in the afterword.

Yellow freckles (*tēmal* etc.), signs of love sickness, are compared to yellow kino flowers. See note on p. 30.

p. 55. Silk-cotton tree: *ilavam*, *ilavu*, a tree with rows of showy scarlet flowers, usually leafless at the time of flowering. The flowers look like cups, the stamens like wicks—hence aptly compared in this poem to the festive rows of lamps lit in the month of Kārttikai (part of November and December). This tall tree grows in dry desert places and hillsides.

p. 59. *ōmai:* toothbrush tree, a reddish tree of the *pālai* desert, where kites and vultures perch; it gives little shade.

I have translated *paṇpu* as "gentle, gentleness." *Paṇpu* means here "nature, quality," as well as "being cultured, well-bred, mature, well-born." Nature and culture meet in this word. The older senses of "gentle" (well-born, well-bred) are not far from *paṇpu*, in itself untranslatable like other central words of a culture.

p. 64. sirissa: *vākai*, tree of the *pālai* landscape, with flowers like peacock crests. The dry pods rattle in the wind.

p. 67. For the characteristics of the *mullai* (jasmine) landscape, see chart 1 in the afterword. The epigraph displays many of the typical motifs: evening, jasmine, loneliness.

p. 69. mound of love: *alkul: mons veneris,* mound of Venus.

p. 70. cassia: *koṉṟai*, also called laburnum. A short tree with bright yellow racemes of flowers, which look like garlands.

p. 76. bilberry tree: *kāyā,* with deep purple flowers.

p. 83. Naḷḷi, one of seven great generous chieftains. Toṇṭi, which belonged to him, is a harbor town on the Cēra (West) coast, known for its cowherds and a white paddy. This harbor was one of the many emporia of ancient Tamil kingdoms mentioned by Greek travel accounts like *The Periplus of the Erythrean Sea.* Note how in this *akam* poem too, proper names are used for special emphatic effects. See note on p. 26.

p. 91. Cow's thorn: *neruñci.*

p. 92. Toṇti city: see note to p. 83.

p. 104. "Goddess of chaste wives": Arundhatī, exemplary wife of one of the Seven Sages, famed for her chastity; one of the stars next to the Big Dipper (called Seven Sages in India). The star is pointed out to new brides during the wedding ceremony.

p. 105. Portia tree: *kāñci.* Barbus fish: *keṇṭai.*

p. 108. For a discussion of this poem see the afterword, section on "Akam and Puṟam as Poetic Devices."

This poem contains one of our earliest descriptions of a Tamil wedding. Some of the features, like the wedding thread, are part of the ritual to this day.

It may be significant that the flora associated with the ritual are the sirissa *(vākai)* from the *pālai* scene (separation, elopement), and *aruku* grass (used in ceremonies) which grows in both *kuṟiñci* (lovers' union) and *mullai* (patient waiting, married happiness). The lily petals *(āmpal)* in her hair grow in the *marutam* pools (lovers' quarrels). These are part of the language of this complex poem on marriage. The happy sensual memory of the wedding night is framed by the infidelity of the man remembering it in the present, when his angry wife (once so docile) has shut the door on him.

p. 111. *Puṟam poems:* The afterword discusses the differences between *akam* and *puṟam* in detail.

See chart 2 on *akam/puṟam* parallels in the afterword.

p. 115. Colophons for *puṟam* or heroic poems mention both the poet and the patron who is the subject or addressee of the poem. *Patiṟṟuppattu* poems like this one are all about Cēra kings ("Cēral"). Only some details regarding poet and patron relevant to the poems will be given here. Over 300 patrons were sung by 144 poets. For brief summaries of what little we know about them, see Subramanian 1966.

p. 116. Poṟai: common Cēra dynastic name. Koṅkar: see note on p. 26.

p. 119. Kiḷḷi is a common Cōḻa dynastic name.

p. 121. Chaplets of palmyra, neem, and laburnum were emblems used by Cēra, Pāṇṭiya, and Cōḻa clans.

This poem and the next one are examples of the poet's role as peacemaker and counsellor.

p. 122. The Cōḻa ancestor (mentioned in the first line) was famous in legend for an extreme act of royal generosity. When a pigeon, hunted by a hawk, sought his protection, he satisfied the hawk's hunger by offering the predator his own flesh in place of the pigeon's.

p. 123. For a discussion of this poem, see the afterword, section on "Two Poems."

p. 125. Pāri: a chieftain. See note on p. 142.

p. 127. An *āṟṟuppaṭai* or "guide poem," in which one poet (minstrel or dancer) leads another to a good patron.

p. 132. "Morning pastorals": songs and tunes appropriate to the *marutam* scene and morning.

"Evening seaside songs": *cevvaḻi* or songs of *neytal*, appropriate to evening.

These are very early references to rāga-like tunes sung only at certain times and places.

p. 135. Crab's-eye: the small *kuṉṟi*, a red seed with a black eye-like dot, used as a jeweler's weight.

p. 137. Cycles of poems praise and mourn seven great chieftains, great warriors and givers. Their gifts to bards and dancers consisted of lotuses made of gold, caparisoned elephants, chariots, whole towns. *Āy* is described as having made himself poor by giving away all he had, all except his women's wedding chains (p. 151).

For more poems by Auvaiyār (the best-known of the classical women poets) on Añci the chieftain, see pp. 139, 167–170.

p. 142. The friendship of Kapilar the brahman poet and Pāri his chieftain is a famous one.

Pāri's generosity was legendary: once, when he saw a jasmine creeper trailing on the ground, he left his chariot there so that the creeper could grow on it. Though he was only a chieftain, he withstood the continual sieges of the three kings (Cēra, Cōḻa, Pāṇṭiya); he finally lost his hill and his life to them (p. 145). After his death, his friend Kapilar found suitable husbands for Pāri's daughters (p. 146).

p. 155. Lessons: There are only about thirteen didactic poems in the anthologies of this period. These few directly express what all the other poems assume.

p. 169. *Where is he now?*: The exclamation *maṉṉe* that occurs six times in this poem expresses sorrow, loss, the passing of things. "Alas, alack, never more, no more" are possible translations, all unsatisfactory. I have taken the liberty of using a line in the poem as a refrain, which says what *maṉṉe* means.

Lemon grass: *narantam*, identified by Cāmi as the "nard" of classical Greek and Latin writers such as Hippocrates, Antiochus, and Pliny. This fragrant grass was used in cookery, perfumes, and drugs. Ancient Greece and Rome imported spices, herbs, and scents from South India at great cost.

pp. 171–72. Neṭuñceḻiyan: The Tamil ideal of a heroic king.

guardian trees: These, like the royal drums, were sacred, emblematic of the rulers of a country. To capture them or cut them down was to vanquish the rulers.

It was customary to sever a warrior's head, as if in battle, before his burial or cremation.

p. 175. Blinding tree: *tillai*. Bindweed: *tāḻi*.

p. 178. A widow lives an austere life, eats lily seed instead of ordinary rice.

p. 180. Except the first, these poems on heroic mothers were by women poets. Ironwood seed: *iravam*.

p. 186. Chaste tree: *nocci*. Its dark green leaves were used by women in love as leaf-skirts (made and given by their lovers), and as emblematic wreaths by warriors during a siege. The poem points to the irony of this double-edged symbol.

p. 188. A king would often ask a chieftain for his daughter's hand. If the chieftain refused, enmity and war would folow. This poem speaks of the destructive power inherent in beautiful women (and in warriors, war drums, etc). Such magical power is *aṇaṅku*, also a goddess. See Hart (1975).

p. 189. See the afterword, section on "Puṟam Poetry," for a comment on this poem. The first few sentences describe the fertility of the kingdoms before they were ravaged by enemies. Canals with fish overflowed into the fields, and often the land was so fertile all they had to do was sow in places where the wild boar had rooted.

she-devil etc: Koṟṟavai, the war goddess, diety of the *pālai* wilderness.

p. 195. These late comic poems are unusual examples of unrequited and mismatched love (the *kaikkiḷai* and *peruntiṇai* genres). See the afterword, "Love Mismatched."

p. 197. In this poem, the woman mocks the lover's (and Tamil poetry's) conventional taffeta phrases, meant to seduce her: especially the riddling hyperboles of stanza 4. Her brow is compared to the moon, shoulders to bamboo, eyes to lotuses, gait to the peacock's, speech to a parrot's—

yet all the metaphors are found wanting, somewhat in the style of Shakespeare's "Shall I compare thee to a summer's day?"

p. 199. gold shark's mouth: a clip-like ornament.

crocus: *naravu*.

p. 203. glory lily: *kāntaḷ*, whose stages of flowering are accurately described here. Also called the "Chinese Lantern" for its colors and shapes.

These flowers blossom with the rains in the *mullai* or pastoral landscape.

bilberry: *kāyā*, the blue flower of the bilberry, is sacred to Kṛṣṇa the cowherd god; the bull-fight contest is also later associated with Kṛṣṇa. Such poems as this, among other things like megaliths, have led some scholars to speculate that the Dravidians must have originally come from Crete and such Mediterranean places.

"The Lord": Śiva.

p. 204. Bhīma, the second of the Pāṇḍava brothers, who ripped apart in an epic battle his cousin and enemy Duśśāsana, for molesting his wife years earlier. A reference to the *Mahābhārata*.

The bull is compared to Śiva, with a moon on his brow. Śiva is also half woman, half man, and an enemy of the Death-god who rides a buffalo.

p. 205. Aśvatthāma, immortal son of Droṇa the brahman warrior, avenges his father's death by going on a crazy murderous rampage. In these folksy poems, the allusions to Sanskrit myths are often wrong. The eunuch killed Bhīṣma, not Droṇa, who was Aśvatthāma's father.

p. 207. I am indebted to David Shulman for leading me to this poem and for sharing his translation of it with me.

p. 209. See the afterword, section on "Love Mismatched," for comments.

p. 210. The love-god Kāma rhymes with Cāma (Skt. Śyāma = Kṛṣṇa) but is not really his brother; the dwarf's ignorance of Sanskrit mythology is part of the comedy.

p. 213. The four pieces in this section barely suggest the upsurge of religious poetry (fifth-sixth century) and its new use of the earlier traditions of love and war. Both Murukaṉ the Red God and Tirumāl the Dark one occur early in Tamil poems as gods of the hillside and the pastoral landscapes. Later, the mythologies of Kumāra (Śiva's son) and Viṣṇu are added to them. The poems in *Paripāṭal* on Tirumāl and Murukaṉ are the earliest bhakti poems in India, the earliest religious poems in a mother tongue. In them, older Sanskritic and Tamil motifs and themes meet and change each other. See Ramanujan 1981, afterword, for a fuller discussion; also Zvelebil 1977, Hardy 1983.

For comments on the epigraph, a short Murukan poem, see the section on "Situations and Frames" in the afterword.

p. 215. This and the last piece (p. 226) are two of the six sections of *Tirumurukāṟṟuppaṭai*, "A Guide to Lord Murukaṉ," which is modeled on an *āṟṟuppaṭai* or guide poem in which one poet leads another to a generous patron (see p. 127 for an example). In this poem, the wandering bards of the earlier tradition have given place to questing devotees; the human patron, to a warrior god. For discussion of this poem, see the afterword.

Like the old chieftains, the god is also associated with certain places. The six sections of the *Guide to Murukaṉ* celebrate six holy places, which are identified with His six faces, thus making Tamil country the body of the god. In this poetic act, the poem, the god, and the country become homologues of one another. This long poem is the first great bhakti poem in Indian literature.

"His Places" is a moving evocation of all the dwelling places of the god. In Tamil bhakti, the divine is immanent in objects.

p. 218. In this short excerpt, we hear a new voice in Tamil poetry—the voice of Sanskritic theology, familiar to readers of texts like the *Bhagavad-gītā*. The Lord here is the essence of all objects: the fragrance in the flower etc. Compare the relatively more Sanskritized Viṣṇu poems here with the Murukaṉ ones.

p. 219. "Hymn to Tirumāl" opens with Sanskritic notions of creation through the aeons, and describes Viṣṇu in terms of his incarnations (the Boar, etc.), his iconography (the wheel in his hand, etc.), but moves on to describe him as a Tamil warrior (p. 221) using *puṟam* imagery. The titles and divisions are mine, and are meant to guide the reader through this early, rather ill-formed, but important poem.

This is probably the earliest *bhakti* poem addressed to Viṣṇu, also one of the first to celebrate a "transcendent" god. See Hardy (1983) on "transcendence" and "immanence."

p. 220. "The conch-colored one": Balarāma, the fair-skinned brother of the dark-skinned Kṛṣṇa.

p. 221. "The Red Goddess": Lakṣmī, whom Viṣṇu bears on his chest. Viṣṇu, in his incarnation as a Boar, rescued the earth goddess from the ocean and married her.

The conch and the discus are two of Viṣṇu's insignia. His body is dark as a blue sapphire; his eyes are compared to lotuses (p. 223); he rides the Garuḍa, the sacred golden eagle, and also carries an emblem of the bird on his banner.

p. 223. The Vedic sacrifice and all its parts are redescribed here as elements of Viṣṇu (who is not prominent in the Vedas).

p. 224. ambrosia: In the myth of the churning of the ocean, Visnu takes on the guise of a beautiful woman and distributes the drink of immortality (*amṛta*, ambrosia) as it rises from the churned waters; partial to the gods, he gives it all to them and deprives and anti-gods of their share.

p. 226. "His Dances," the fifth section of *A Guide to Lord Murukaṉ*, evokes a community, joyous, erotic, dancing, with a shaman in their midst who wears the Red One's insignia (his lance, red robes) and becomes Him. The wreaths, the flora, the imagery, the musical instruments are all properties from the older *kuṟiñci* love poems, for Murukaṉ is the god of the *kuṟiñci* or hillside landscape. He is the god of love, war, fertility, youth.

The last lines, "His being there, and not only there," contain the quintessence of bhakti.

An earlier version of "His Dances" appeared in *Hymns for the Drowning* (Ramanujan 1981:112–15), copyright © 1981 by Princeton University Press, revised and reprinted here by permission of the publisher.

Notes to the Afterword

1. Portions of this afterword have appeared in earlier versions in the following: *The Interior Landscape* (Bloomington, 1967 now out of print); lecture at the University of Texas, 1968, later published as "Form in Classical Tamil Poetry" in *Symposium on Dravidian Civilization*, ed. Andree Sjoberg (Austin, 1971); "Towards an Anthology of Indian City Images," in Richard Fox, ed., *Urban India: Society, Space and Image* (Durham, 1970); "Nature and Culture in Indian Poetry," lecture at University of California, Berkeley, 1972.

2. The reader might be interested in looking at the original (which appears in Tamil characters opposite the English poem):

aṉṉāy vāḻivēṇ ṭaṉṉainam paṭappait
tēṉmayaṅku pāliṉu miṉiya vavarnāṭ
ṭuvalaik kūvaṟ kīḻa
māṉuṇ ṭeñciya kaḻili nīrē

If we separate and display the meaningful units, we see:

aṉṉāy vāḻi vēṇṭ(u) aṉṉai[A] / nam paṭappai-t-
tēṉ - mayaṅku - pāl - iṉum iṉiya[B] / (v)avar nāṭ-
ṭ(u) uvalai-k-kūval - kīḻa
māṉ - uṇṭ(u) - eñciya kaḻili nīrē[C] /

The translation, piece by piece, would be:

mother, may(-you)-live, desire (to listen), mother[A] / our garden-
honey-mixed-milk-than sweet(er)[B] / (is) his land's,
(in-) leaf-holes-low,
animals-having-drunk-(and)leftover, muddied water[C] /

The poem is in *akaval* meter, like most of these poems—four quantitative feet to every line (see note 12), except the penultimate, which has only three, indicated by spaces in the first citation. The lines are not end-stopped, i.e., they do not always coincide with the end of a sentence or clause, often not even with the end of a word, as in the second line. The lines are held together usually by the second consonant of each line, in a kind of rhyme or chime: here, lines 1, 2, and 4 have *n* as the second consonant; they are enriched by alliterations *(v . . . v)*, assonances *(avar, uvalai, kūval)*, rhymes *(vēṇṭu/uṇṭu;* or *iṉiya/eñciya)*, and a dense pattern of consonants, e.g., nasals occur 19 times, deepening our sense of the central word *(-iṉum)iṉiya*, "sweet(er) than," which is the syntactic pivot of the poem.

The grammatical form, *B than sweeter (is) C*, postpones C, the subject of the comparison which is also the subject of the whole poem (*nīr*, "water") to the very end, making us wait for it—creating a kind of syntactic suspense. Such suspense is achieved by a deft use of the relatively free word order and the "left-branching" syntax of Tamil: for instance, in ordinary English the main sentence will have to be *C is sweeter than B*, which is exactly the reverse of the Tamil sequence. In left-branching languages like Tamil, verbs come at the end of the sentence, objects and adjectival clauses before predicates (e.g., the whole phrase in C), adverbials before verbs; case-endings and particles occur after rather than before what they govern. An English sentence like *He is taller than you* translates in Tamil as *You-than he tall(er) is)*. The relatively free order allows "he" to move to the beginning or the end of the Tamil sentence.

Dylan Thomas's (or Hopkins's) left-branching, Welsh-like noun phrases, as in "Never until *the mankind making bird beast and flower / fathering all-humbling darkness*," could be translated in exactly the same order in ordinary Tamil (and some other Indian languages).

If poetry is made out of, among other things, "the best words in the best order" and the best orders of two languages are the reverse mirror images of each other, what is a translator to do? Many of my devices (e.g., indentation, spacing) and compromises are made in order to mimic closely the syntactic suspense of the original, without, I hope, estranging English. Often, the poems unify their rich and diverse associations by using a single long marvellously managed sentence.

3. This fact adds further subtlety to the symbolism. *Pālai* (wasteland) associated with separation can happen even in the heart of union (*kuṟiñci* or mountain landscape).

4. "Objective correlatives" (Eliot 1950), and what I have called correlative objects, are very different things: the first are sought and found by individual poets, the latter are given by the culture in which the poets dwell.

5. From now on, I translate *tiṇai* as "landscape." But *tiṇai* has several meanings: "class, genre, type", as in *akattiṇai* "the *akam* genre." In a more specific sense, *tiṇai* is a complex concept defined in the poetics for Tamil poetry: a genre is represented by a region or landscape, its nature and culture, and the human feelings associated with them—in short, an entire ecosystem used for poetic expression. "Landscape" is a convenient metonymy for the whole cluster of notions. Like the Tamils, we will also use the names *kuṟiñci*, *mullai* etc. for the landscapes and the genres associated with them.

6. This series is clearly reminiscent of the Jain "ladder of life" of *ekendriya* ("one sense"), *dvendriya* ("two-sense"), etc., all the way to the gods. See Zimmer (1960:277) for an exposition of this Jain system. Though several such Jain elements are found or "borrowed" in the Tamil texts, their use is not Jain at all; its

thrust is not metaphysical, religious, nor does it imply an ethic of nonviolence. Instead, it adds one more "concrete" figure to the poetry. The subject of Jain ideas in early Tamil literature merits exploration.

7. My use of "metaphor" and "metonymy" follows Jakobson (1971:254–7), whom I find suggestive. As I show below, the categories cannot be mutually exclusive, nor can all figures be divided into these two super-classes. For a cogent criticism, see Genette (1982).

8. This section, while it disagrees in some matters with Kailasapathy, is deeply indebted to his exposition.

9. For a critical discussion of Milman Parry's antecedents and influence on Homeric scholarship, and the dozens of later studies accepting, rejecting or modifying and extending his ideas—see Adam Parry's introduction to Parry (1971). Parry's work on the formula dates from 1928. See also Stolz and Shannon (1976) for recent discussions.

10. Kailasapathy (1968:162–63) lists 121 such recurrent epithets for Tamil.

11. Oral epics are currently being collected and studied in several Dravidian languages: by Brenda Beck, Stuart Blackburn, and N. Vanamamalai in Tamil, Peter Claus in Tulu, Gene Roghair and V. Narayana Rao in Telugu, G. S. Paramasivayya and others in Kannaḍa.

12. Tamil meter has many kinds of feet *(cīr)* that make up a line *(aṭi)*. A foot consists of syllabic patterns *(acai)* which may contain one long syllable (*nēr*: consonant—long vowel—consonant or CV̄C) or two short syllables (*nirai*: CV̆-CV̆).

The classical *akaval* meter, for instance, has two *acai*'s in a foot, with four possible kinds of foot: *nēr nēr* CV̄C CV̄C, *nirai nēr* CV̆CV̆ CV̄C, *nēr nirai* CV̄C CV̆CV̆, *nirai nirai* CV̆CV̆ CV̆CV̆. An *akaval* line has four such feet in a line, except in the penultimate line (of a poem) which has only three.

But metrical length does not always coincide with actual vowel length. A vowel is considered metrically "long" if (a) it is a long vowel, or (b) it is in a closed syllable. A short syllable is considered "long" if it occurs alone, or if it is the last syllable of a foot. If the first syllable of a foot is short, the next one is considered "short," whatever its actual length. When a word-final u occurs in a *nirai*, it is called *niraipu*.

As in every metrical system, the actual scanning of a line is complex; it requires rules, precedents, and a good ear.

Here is a standard illustration which has examples of all the above metrical considerations:

nirai	nēr	nirai	nēr	nirai	nēr	nēr	nēr	nēr
aka	*ra*	*muta*	*la*	*eḻut*	*tel*	*lām*	*ā*	*ti*

nirai	nēr	nirai	nēr	niraipu
paka	*vaṉ*	*mutaṟ*	*ṟe*	*ulaku*

Appendix

Plant Names

English	*Tamil*	*Latin*
asoka	*acōkam*	*Saraca indica*
bilberry	*kāyā*	*Memecylon edule*
black babul	*uṭai*	*Acacia eburnia*
blinding tree	*tillai*	*Exocoeria agallocha*
cadamba oak	*kaṭampu*	*Anthocephalus cadamba*
cassia	*koṉṟai*	*Cassia fistula etc.*
chaste tree	*nocci*	*Vitex agnus-castus*
conehead	*kuṟiñci*	*Strobilanthes (genus)*
cow's thorn	*neruñci*	*Terrestris tribulis*
crab's eye	*kuṉṟi*	*Abrus precatoris*
creeping bindweed	*vaḷḷai*	*Ipomaea aquatica*
crocus	*naṟavu*	*Crocus sativus*
dark lily	*neytal*	*Nymphae stellata*
glory lily	*kāntaḷ*	*Gloriosa superba*
hedge bindweed	*tāḷi*	*Ipomaea sepiaria*
ironwood	*iravam*	*Mesua ferrea*
ivorywood tree	*pālai*	*Wrightia tinctoria*
jackfruit	*palavu*	*Artocarpus integriforia*
jalap	*pakaṉṟai*	*Exogonium purga*

kino tree	*vēṅkai*	*Pterocarpus marsupium*
laburnum, *see* cassia		
laurel (Alexandrian)	*puṉṉai*	*Calophyllum inophyllum*
mastwood, *see* laurel		
neem tree	*vēmpu*	*Melia azadirachta*
nightshade	*kūtaḷi*	*Solanum trilobatum*
portia	*kāñci*	*Trewia nudiflora*
queen's-flower	*marutam*	*Lagerstroemia flos-regina*
screwpine	*tāḻai*	*Pandanus odoritissimus*
silk cotton tree	*ilavam*	*Bombax malabaricum*
sirissa	*vākai*	*Albizzia*
sweet basil	*karantai*	*Ocimum* (genus)
sweet potato, *see* yam		
thorny babul	*viṭattēr(ai)*	*Dichrostachys cineria*
tigerclaw tree	*ñāḻal, pulinakak-koṉṟai*	*Cassia sophera* (fetid cassia)
toothbrush tree	*ōmai*	?
water thorn	*muṇṭakam*	?
white dead nettle	*tumpai*	*Leucas* (genus)
white lily	*āmpal*	*Nymphaea lotus alba*
whortleberry	*kaḷā*	*Vaccinium nilgherrense*
wild jasmine	*piṭavam*	?
yam	*vaḷḷi*	*Dioscorea sativa?*

Familiar names like bamboo, mango, jasmine are not included in this list.

References

Tamil Sources

Aiṅkuṟunūṟu. 1957. With an old commentary, edited by U. Vē. Cāminātaiyar. 5th ed. Madras: Kapīr Accukkūṭam.

——. 1957–58. Edited with a commentary by Auvai C. Turaicāmippiḷḷai. 3 vols. Annamalai: Annamalai University.

——. 1966. Edited with a commentary by P. V. Cōmacuntaraṉār. Madras: Kaḻakam.

Akanāṉūṟu. 1965. Edited with a commentary by N. M. Veṅkaṭacāmi Nāṭṭār and R. Veṅkaṭācalam Piḷḷai. Madras: Kaḻakam.

Kalittokai. 1967. Old commentary by Nacciṉārkkiṉiyar. Madras: Kaḻakam.

Kuṟuntokai. 1962. Edited with a commentary by U. Vē. Cāminātaiyar. 4th ed. Madras: Kapīr Accukkūṭam.

Naṟṟiṇai. 1962. Edited with a commentary by A. Nārāyaṇacāmi Aiyar. Madras: Kaḻakam.

——. 1966–68. Edited with a commentary by Auvai C. Turaicāmippiḷḷai. 2 vols. Madras: Aruṇā Publications.

Paripāṭal. 1956. With an old commentary by Parimēlaḻakar, edited by U. Vē. Cāminātaiyar. 4th ed. Madras: Kapīr Accukkūṭam.

——. 1964. Edited with a commentary by P. V. Cōmacuntaraṉār. Madras: Kaḻakam.

Patiṟṟuppattu. 1957. With an old commentary, edited by U. Vē. Cāminātaiyar. 6th ed. Madras: Kapīr Accukkūṭam.

——. 1963. Edited with a commentary by Auvai C. Turāicamippiḷḷai. Madras: Kaḻakam.

Pattuppāṭṭu. 1961. With an old commentary by Naccinārkkiniyar, edited by U. Vē. Cāminātaiyar. 6th ed. Madras: Kapīr Accukkūṭam.

——. 1966. Edited with a commentary by P. V. Cōmacuntaraṉār, 2 vols. Madras: Kaḻakam.

Puṟanāṉūṟu. 1962, 1967. Edited with a commentary by Auvai C. Turaicāmippiḷḷai, 2 vols. Madras: Kaḻakam.

——. 1963. With an old commentary, edited by U. Vē. Cāmiṉātaiyar, 6th ed. Madras: Kapīr Accukkūṭam.

Tolkāppiyam, Poruḷatikāram. n.d. Old commentary by Nacciṉārkkiṉiyar. 3 vols. Madras: Kaḻakam.

——. 1961. Old Commentary by Pērāciriyar. Madras: Kaḻakam.

Vaiyāpuri Piḷḷai, S. 1940. *Caṅka Ilakkiyam, Pāṭṭum Tokaiyum*. Madras. (First edition.)

Lexicons, Indexes etc.

Burrow, T. and M. B. Emeneau. 1960. *A Dravidian Etymological Dictionary*. London: Oxford University Press.

Cañcīvi, Na. 1973. *Caṅka Ilakkiya Ārāycci Aṭṭavaṇaikaḷ*. Madras: University of Madras.

Index des mots de la litterature tamoule ancienne. 1967–. Pondichéry: Institut Français d'Indologie.

Subramanian, N. 1966. *Pre-Pallavan Tamil Index*. Madras: University of Madras.

Subramoniam, V. I. 1962. *Index of Puṟanaaṉuuṟu*. Trivandrum: University of Kerala.

Tamil Lexicon. 1936. 6 vols. Madras: University of Madras. Supplement, 1938.

Some Translations from Classical Tamil

Chellaiya, J. V. 1962. *Pattuppāṭṭu* (Ten Tamil Idylls). Madras: Kaḻakam.

Gros, Francois. 1968. *Le Paripāṭal*. Pondichéry: Institut Français d'Indologie.

Hart, George L. III. 1979. *Poets of the Tamil Anthologies*. Princeton: Princeton University Press.

Ilakkuvanar, S. 1963. *Tholkappiyam (in English)*. Madurai: Kuṟaḷ Neṟi Publishing House.

Ramanujan, A. K. 1967. *The Interior Landscape*. Bloomington: Indiana University Press.

See also, Basham 1950, Hart 1975, Kailasapathy 1968, Zvelebil 1973 and 1974.

Other Works

Barthes, Roland. 1967. *Elements of Semiology*, tr. from the French by Annette Lavers and Colin Smith. London: Cape.

Basham, A. L. 1959. *The Wonder That Was India*. New York: Grove Press.

Bloom, Harold. 1973. *The Anxiety of Influence*. New York: Oxford University Press.

Bowra, C. M. 1952. *Heroic Poetry*. London: Macmillan.

Burke, Kenneth. 1945. *A Grammar of Motives*. New York: Prentice-Hall.

Cāmi, P. L. 1967. *Caṅka Ilakkiyattil Ceṭikoṭi Viḷakkam*. Tinnevelly: South Indian Saiva Siddhanta Works Publishing Society.

——. 1970. *Caṅka Ilakkiyattil Viḷaṅkiṉa Viḷakkam*. Tinnevelly: South Indian Saiva Siddhanta Works Publishing Society.

Cāminātaiyar, U. Vē. 1950. *Eṉ Carittiram*. Madras.

Chadwick, N. K. 1942. *Poetry and Prophecy*. Cambridge: Cambridge University Press.

Chadwick, H. M. and N. K. Chadwick. 1932–40. *The Growth of Literature*. 3 vols. New York: Macmillan.

Clothey, Fred W. 1978. *The Many Faces of Murugan*. New York: Mouton.

Crane, Robert I., ed. 1970. *Transition in South Asia: Problems of Modernization*. Monograph Series. Durham, N. C.: Duke University.

Culley, Robert C. 1967. *Oral Formulaic Language in the Biblical Psalms*. Toronto: University of Toronto Press.

Eliot, T. S. 1950. *Selected Essays*. New York: Harcourt, Brace.

Fox, Richard G., ed. 1970. *Urban India: Society, Space, and Image*. Monograph Series. Durham, N. C.: Duke University.

Gamble, J. S. 1957. *Flora of the Presidency of Madras*. Calcutta: Botanical Survey of India.

Genette, Gerard. 1982. *Figures of Literary Discourse*, tr. by Alan Sheridan. New York: Columbia University Press.

Hardy, Friedhelm. 1983. *Viraha Bhakti: The Early History of Kṛṣna Devotion in South India*. Delhi: Oxford University Press.

Hart, George L. III. 1975. *The Poems of Ancient Tamil*. Berkeley: University of California Press.

Ingalls, Daniel H. H. 1965. *An Anthology of Sanskrit Court Poetry*. Cambridge: Harvard University Press.

Jakobson, Roman. 1971. *Selected Writings II*. The Hague: Mouton.

Kailasapathy, K. 1968. *Tamil Heroic Poetry*. Oxford: Clarendon Press.

Levi-Strauss, Claude. 1966. *The Savage Mind*. Chicago: University of Chicago Press.

—— 1969. *The Raw and the Cooked*, tr. by John and Doreen Weightman. New York: Harper and Row.

Lord, A. B. 1960. *The Singer of Tales*. Cambridge: Harvard University Press.

Moore, Marianne. 1951. *Collected Poems*. New York: Macmillan.
Nagler, Michael N. 1974. *Spontaneity and Tradition: A Study in the Oral Art of Homer*. Berkeley: University of California Press.
Nilakanta Sastry, K. A. 1966. *A History of South India*. 3d ed. Madras: Oxford University Press.
Parry, Milman. 1971. *The Making of Homeric Verse: The Collected Papers of Milman Parry*, ed. by Adam Parry. Oxford: Clarendon Press.
Perse, St.-John. 1966. *Birds*, tr. by R. Fitzgerald. New York: Pantheon Books.
Ramanujan, A. K. 1970a. "Towards an Anthology of City Images." In Richard G. Fox, ed., *Urban India: Society, Space, and Image*. Monograph Series. Durham, N. C.: Duke University.
—— 1970b. "Language and Social Change." In Robert I. Crane, ed., *Transition in South Asia: Problems of Modernization*. Monograph Series. Durham, N. C.: Duke University.
—— 1981. *Hymns for the Drowning: Poems of Nammalvar*. Princeton: Princeton University Press.
—— 1985. "Two Realms of Kannada Folklore." In Stuart Blackburn and A. K. Ramanujan, eds., *Another Harmony: New Essays in the Folklore of India*. Berkeley: University of California Press.
Saussure, Ferdinand de. 1959. *Course in General Linguistics*, tr. by Wade Baskin. New York: McGraw-Hill.
Singaravelu, S. 1966. *Social Life of the Tamils: The Classical Period*. Kuala Lumpur: University of Malaya.
Shulman, David. 1980. *Tamil Temple Myths*. Princeton: Princeton University Press.
Sjoberg, Andrée, ed. 1971. *Symposium on Dravidian Civilization*. Austin: Jenkins.
Stolz, Benjamin A. and Richard S. Shannon, eds. 1976. *Oral Literature and the Formula*. Ann Arbor: University of Michigan.
Subramanian, N. 1966. *Sangam Polity*. Bombay: Asia Publishing House.
Varadarajan, M. 1969. *The Treatment of Nature in Sangam Literature*. 2d ed. Tinnevelly: South Indian Saiva Siddhanta Works Publishing Society.
Wang, Ching-hsien. 1971. "Formulaic Language and Mode of Creation." Ph.D. diss., University of California, Berkeley.
Zimmer, Heinrich. 1960. *Philosophies of India*, ed. by Joseph Campbell. New York: Meridian Books.
Zvelebil, K. V. 1973. *The Smile of Murugan*. Leiden: Brill, 1973.
—— 1974. *Tamil Literature*. Weisbaden: Harrassowitz.
—— 1977. "The Beginnings of Bhakti in South India." *Temenos*, 13:223–57.

Index of Poets

The poets' names tell us many things about them. Ālattūr Kiḻār means "Kiḻār of Ālattūr" (indicates place-name); Āciriyaṉ Peruṅkaṇṇaṉ, "Teacher named Big Kaṇṇaṉ" or "Teacher Big-Eyes" (profession, and a physical characteristic); Uruttiraṉār, "Rudra" (name of Śiva, obviously a Śiva-worshiper's name); Māmūlaṉār, "Great Mūlam-man," (Mūlam is the name of a star; maybe the poet's birth star?); Pālaipāṭiya Peruṅkaṭuṅkō, "The Great Hard King who sang *pālai* songs" (the genre he specialized in); Āvūrkiḻār Makaṉār Kaṇṇaṉār, "Kaṇṇaṉ, son of Kiḻār of Āvūr" (his father's name); Kuṟamakaḷ Iḷaveyiṉi "Young Veyiṉi, woman of the Kuṟava hill tribe" (name of clan, caste, or tribe); Auvaiyār, "Mother" (gender); Ōrampōkiyār, "One Who Walks on the edge?" (characteristic behavior); Pālaipāṭiya Peruṅkaṭuṅkō, "Great Hard King Who sang *pālai* songs" (class, here, the poet is a king); Pūṅkaṇṇaṉ, "Flower-eyed man" (Kaṇṇaṉ, one among twenty names common at the time; 34 poets' names include Kaṇṇaṉ in them). Later, of course, Kaṇṇaṉ was the Tamil form of Kṛṣṇa. Twenty-seven poets are named after a phrase they made, e.g., Cempulappeyaṉīrār, "Poet of the red earth and pouring rain." The *-ār* suffix at the end of many names is an honorific.

Twelve of these are women poets: Auvaiyār. Aḷḷūr Naṉmullai, Kākkai Pāṭiṉiyār Nacceḷḷaiyār, Kāvaṟpeṇṭu, Kuṟamakaḷ Iḷaveyiṉi, Mārippittiyār, Nakkaṇṇaiyār, Naṉṉākaiyār, Pari's Daughters, Pūṅkaṇuttiraiyār, Veḷḷi Vītiyār and Veṟipāṭiya Kāmakkaṇṇiyār.

Curious readers may consult Subramanian (1966), for brief notes on all the poets and their patrons.

Index of Titles and First Lines

(Titles are in bold type; titles like *What She Said* are not included)

Other Works in the Columbia Asian Studies Series

TRANSLATIONS FROM THE ASIAN CLASSICS

Major Plays of Chikamatsu, tr. Donald Keene 1961

Four Major Plays of Chikamatsu, tr. Donald Keene. Paperback ed. only. 1961; rev. ed. 1997

Records of the Grand Historian of China, translated from the Shih chi of Ssu-ma Ch'ien, tr. Burton Watson, 2 vols. 1961

Instructions for Practical Living and Other Neo-Confucian Writings by Wang Yang-ming, tr. Wing-tsit Chan 1963

Hsün Tzu: Basic Writings, tr. Burton Watson, paperback ed. only. 1963; rev. ed. 1996

Chuang Tzu: Basic Writings, tr. Burton Watson, paperback ed. only. 1964; rev. ed. 1996

The Mahābhārata, tr. Chakravarthi V. Narasimhan. Also in paperback ed. 1965; rev. ed. 1997

The Manyōshū, Nippon Gakujutsu Shinkōkai edition 1965

Su Tung-p'o: Selections from a Sung Dynasty Poet, tr. Burton Watson. Also in paperback ed. 1965

Bhartrihari: Poems, tr. Barbara Stoler Miller. Also in paperback ed. 1967

Basic Writings of Mo Tzu, Hsün Tzu, and Han Fei Tzu, tr. Burton Watson. Also in separate paperback eds. 1967

The Awakening of Faith, Attributed to Aśvaghosha, tr. Yoshito S. Hakeda. Also in paperback ed. 1967

Reflections on Things at Hand: The Neo-Confucian Anthology, comp. Chu Hsi and Lii Tsu-ch'ien, tr. Wing-tsit Chan 1967
The Platform Sutra of the Sixth Patriarch, tr. Philip B. Yampolsky. Also in paperback ed. 1967
Essays in Idleness: The Tsurezuregusa of Kenkō, tr. Donald Keene. Also in paperback ed. 1967
The Pillow Book of Sei Shōnagon, tr. Ivan Morris, 2 vols. 1967
Two Plays of Ancient India: The Little Clay Cart and the Minister's Seal, tr. J. A. B. van Buitenen 1968
The Complete Works of C.huang Tzu, tr. Burton Watson 1968
The Romance of the Western Chamber (Hsi Hsiang chi), tr. S. I. Hsiung. Also in paperback ed. 1968
The Manyōshū, Nippon Gakujutsu Shinkōkai edition. Paperback ed. only. 1969
Records of the Historian: Chapters from the Shih chi of Ssu-ma Ch'ien, tr. Burton Watson. Paperback ed. only. 1969
Cold Mountain: 100 Poems by the T'ang Poet Han-shan, tr. Burton Watson. Also in paperback ed. 1970
Twenty Plays of the Nō Theatre, ed. Donald Keene. Also in paperback ed. 1970
Chūshingura: The Treasury. of Loyal Retainers, tr. Donald Keene. Also in paperback ed. 1971; rev. ed. 1997
The Zen Master Hakuin: Selected Writings, tr. Philip B. Yampolsky 1971
Chinese Rhyme-Prose: Poems in the Fu Form from the Han and Six Dynasties Periods, tr. Burton Watson. Also in paperback ed. 1971
Kūkai: Major Works, tr. Yoshito S. Hakeda. Also in paperback ed. 1972
The Old Man Who Does as He Pleases: Selections from the Poetry and Prose of Luyu, tr. Burton Watson 1973
The Lion's Roar of Queen Śrīmālā, tr. Alex and Hideko Wayman 1974
Courtier and Commoner in Ancient China: Selections from the History of the Former Han by pan Ku, tr. Burton Watson. Also in paperback ed. 1974
Japanese Literature in Chinese, vol. 1: *Poetry and Prose in Chinese by Japanese Writers of the Early Period*, tr. Burton Watson 1975
Japanese Literature in Chinese, vol. 2: *Poet .ry and Prose in Chinese by Japanese Writers of the Later Period*, tr. Burton Watson 1976
Scripture of the Lotus Blossom of the Fine Dharma, tr. Leon Hurvitz. Also in paperback ed. 1976
Love Song of the Dark Lord: Jayadeva's *Gītagovinda*, tr. Barbara Stoler Miller. Also in paperback ed. Cloth ed. includes critical text of the Sanskrit. 1977; rev. ed. 1997
Ryōkan: Zen Monk-Poet of Japan, tr. Burton Watson 1977

Calming the Mind and Discerning the Real: From the Lam rim chen mo of Tsoṇ-kha-pa, tr. Alex Wayman 1978
The Hermit and the Love-Thief: Sanskrit Poems of Bhartrihari and Bilhaṇa, tr. Barbara Stoler Miller 1978
The Lute: Kao Ming's P'i-p'a chi, tr. Jean Mulligan. Also in paperback ed. 1980
A Chronicle of Gods and Sovereigns: Jinnō Shōtōki of Kitabatake Chikafusa, tr. H. Paul Varley 1980
Among the Flowers: The Hua-chien chi, tr. Lois Fusek 1982
Grass Hill: Poems and Prose by the Japanese Monk Gensei, tr. Burton Watson 1983
Doctors, Diviners, and Magicians of Ancient China: Biographies of Fang-shih, tr. Kenneth J. DeWoskin. Also in paperback ed. 1983
Theater of Memory: The Plays of Kālidāsa, ed. Barbara Stoler Miller. Also in paperback ed. 1984
The Columbia Book of Chinese Poetry: From Early Times to the Thirteenth Century, ed. and tr. Burton Watson. Also in paperback ed. 1984
Poems of Love and War: From the Eight Anthologies and the Ten Long Poems of Classical Tamil, tr. A. K. Ramanujan. Also in paperback ed. 1985
The Bhagavad Gita: Krishna's Counsel in Time of War, tr. Barbara Stoler Miller 1986
The Columbia Book of Later Chinese Poetry, ed. and tr. Jonathan Chaves. Also in paperback ed. 1986
The Tso Chuan: Selections from China's Oldest Narrative History, tr. Burton Watson 1989
Waiting for the Wind: Thirty-six Poets of Japan's Late Medieval Age, tr. Steven Carter 1989
Selected Writings of Nichiren, ed. Philip B. Yampolsky 1990
Saigyō, Poems of a Mountain Home, tr. Burton Watson 1990
The Book of Lieh Tzu: A Classic of the Tao, tr. A. C. Graham. Morningside ed. 1990
The Tale of an Anklet: An Epic of South India—The Cilappatikāram of Iḷaṅkō Aṭikaḷ, tr. R. Parthasarathy 1993
Waiting for the Dawn: A Plan for the Prince, tr. and introduction by Wm. Theodore de Bary 1993
Yoshitsune and the Thousand Cherry Trees: A Masterpiece of the Eighteenth-Century Japanese Puppet Theater, tr. annotated, and with introduction by Stanleigh H. Jones, Jr. 1993
The Lotus Sutra, tr. Burton Watson. Also in paperback ed. 1993

The Classic of Changes: A New Translation of the I Ching as Interpreted by Wang Bi, tr. Richard John Lynn 1984
Beyond Spring: Tz'u Poems of the Sung Dynasty, tr. Julie Landau 1994
The Columbia Anthology of Traditional Chinese Literature, ed. Victor H. Mair 1994
Scenes for Mandarins: The Elite Theater of the Ming, tr. Cyril Birch 1995
Letters of Nichiren, ed. Philip B. Yampolsky; tr. Burton Watson et al. 1996
Unforgotten Dreams: Poems by the Zen Monk Shōtetsu, tr. Steven D. Carter 1997
The Vimalakirti Sutra, tr. Burton Watson 1997
Japanese and Chinese Poems to Sing: The Wakan rōei shū, tr. J. Thomas Rimer and Jonathan Chaves 1997
Breeze Through Bamboo: Kanshi of Ema Saikō, tr. Hiroaki Sato 1998
A Tower for the Summer Heat, Li Yu, tr. Patrick Hanan 1998
Traditional Japanese Theater: An Anthology of Plays, Karen Brazell 1998
The Original Analects: Sayings of Confucius and His Successors (0479–0249), E. Bruce Brooks and A. Taeko Brooks 1998
The Classic of the Way and Virtue: A New Translation of the Tao-te ching *of Laozi as Interpreted by Wang Bi*, tr. Richard John Lynn 1999
The Four Hundred Songs of War and Wisdom: An Anthology of Poems from Classical Tamil, The Puranāṇūṛu, ed. and trans. George L. Hart and Hank Heifetz 1999
Original Tao: Inward Training (Nei-yeh) *and the Foundations of Taoist Mysticism*, by Harold D. Roth 1999
Lao Tzu's Tao Te Ching: *A Translation of the Startling New Documents Found at Guodian*, Robert G. Henricks 2000
The Shorter Columbia Anthology of Traditional Chinese Literature, ed. Victor H. Mair 2000
Mistress and Maid (Jiaohongji) by Meng Chengshun, tr. Cyril Birch 2001
Chikamatsu: Five Late Plays, tr. and ed. C. Andrew Gerstle 2001
The Essential Lotus: Selections from the Lotus Sutra, tr. Burton Watson 2002
Early Modern Japanese Literature: An Anthology., 1600–1900, ed. Haruo Shirane 2002
The Sound of the Kiss, or The Story. That Must Never Be Told: Pingali Suranna's Kalapurnodayamu, tr. Vecheru Narayana Rao and David Shulman 2003
The Selected Poems of Du Fu, tr. Burton Watson 2003
Far Beyond the Field: Haiku by Japanese Women, tr. Makoto Ueda 2003

Just Living: Poems and Prose by the Japanese Monk Tonna, ed. and tr. Steven D. Carter 2003
Han Feizi: Basic Writings, tr. Burton Watson 2003
Mozi: Basic Writings, tr. Burton Watson 2003
Xunzi: Basic Writings, tr. Burton Watson 2003
Zhuangzhi: Basic Writings, tr. Burton Watson 2003

MODERN ASIAN LITERATURE

Modern Japanese Drama: An Anthology, ed. and tr. Ted. Takaya. Also in paperback ed. 1979
Mask and Sword: Two Plays for the Contemporary. Japanese Theater, by Yamazaki Masakazu, tr. J. Thomas Rimer 1980
Yokomitsu Riichi, Modernist, Dennis Keene 1980
Nepali Visions, Nepali Dreams: The Poetry. of Laxmiprasad Devkota, tr. David Rubin 1980
Literature of the Hundred Flowers, vol. 1: *Criticism and Polemics*, ed. Hualing Nieh 1981
Literature of the Hundred Flowers, vol. 2: *Poetry and Fiction*, ed. Hualing Nieh 1981
Modern Chinese Stories and Novellas, 1919–1949, ed. Joseph S. M. Lau, C. T. Hsia, and Leo Ou-fan Lee. Also in paperback ed. 1984
A View by the Sea, by Yasuoka Shōtarō, tr. Kären Wigen Lewis 1984
Other Worlds: Arishima Takeo and the Bounds of Modern Japanese Fiction, by Paul Anderer 1984
Selected Poems of Sō Chōngju, tr. with introduction by David R. McCann 1989
The Sting of Life: Four Contemporary Japanese Novelists, by Van C. Gessel 1989
Stories of Osaka Life, by Oda Sakunosuke, tr. Burton Watson 1990
The Bodhisattva, or Samantabhadra, by Ishikawa Jun, tr. with introduction by William Jefferson Tyler 1990
The Travels of Lao Ts'an, by Liu T'ieh-yün, tr. Harold Shadick, Morningside ed. 1990
Three Plays by Kōbō Abe, tr. with introduction by Donald Keene 1993
The Columbia Anthology of Modern Chinese Literature, ed. Joseph S. M. Lau and Howard Goldblatt 1995
Modern Japanese Tanka, ed. and tr. by Makoto Ueda 1996
Masaoka Shiki: Selected Poems, ed. and tr. by Burton Watson 1997
Writing Women in Modern China: An Anthology of Women's Literature from the Early Twentieth Century, ed. and tr. by Amy D. Dooling and Kristina M. Torgeson 1998
American Stories, by Nagai Kafū, tr. Mitsuko Iriye 2000

The Paper Door and Other Stories, by Shiga Naoya, tr. Lane Dunlop 2001
Grass for My Pillow, by Saiichi Maruya, tr. Dennis Keene 2002
For All My Walking: Free-Verse Haiku of Taneda Santōka, with Excerpts from His Diaries, tr. Burton Watson 2003

STUDIES IN ASIAN CULTURE

The Ōnin War: History of Its Origins and Background, with a Selective Translation of the Chronicle of Ōnin, by H. Paul Varley 1967
Chinese Government in Ming Times: Seven Studies, ed. Charles O. Hucker 1969
The Actors' Analects (Yakusha Rongo), ed. and tr. by Charles J. Dunn and Bungō Torigoe 1969
Self and Society in Ming Thought, by Wm. Theodore de Bary and the Conference on Ming Thought. Also in paperback ed. 1970
A History. of Islamic Philosophy, by Majid Fakhry, 2d ed. 1983
Phantasies of a Love Thief: The Caurapañatcāsikā Attributed to Bilhaṇa, by Barbara Stoler Miller 1971
Iqbal: Poet-Philosopher of Pakistan, ed. Hafeez Malik 1971
The Golden Tradition: An Anthology of Urdu Poetry, ed. and tr. Ahmed Ali. Also in paperback ed. 1973
Conquerors and Confucians: Aspects of Political Change in Late Yiian China, by John W. Dardess 1973
The Unfolding of Neo-Confucianism, by Wm. Theodore de Bary and the Conference on Seventeenth-Century Chinese Thought. Also in paperback ed. 1975
To Acquire Wisdom: The Way of Wang Yang-ming, by Julia Ching 1976
Gods, Priests, and Warriors: The Bhṛgus of the Mahābhārata, by Robert P. Goldman 1977
Mei Yao-ch'en and the Development of Early SungPoetry, by Jonathan Chaves 1976
The Legend of Semimaru, Blind Musician of Japan, by Susan Matisoff 1977
Sir Sayyid Ahmad Khan and Muslim Modernization in India and Pakistan, by Hafeez Malik 1980
The Khilafat Movement: Religious Symbolism and Political Mobilization in India, by Gall Minault 1982
The World of K'ung Shang-jen: A Man of Letters in Early Ch'ing China, by Richard Strassberg 1983
The Lotus Boat: The Origins of Chinese Tz'u Poetry in T'ang Popular Culture, by Marsha L. Wagner 1984

Expressions of Self in Chinese Literature, ed. Robert E. Hegel and Richard C. Hessney 1985
Songs for the Bride: Women's Voices and Wedding Rites of Rural India, by W. G. Archer; ed. Barbara Stoler Miller and Mildred Archer 1986
The Confucian Kingship in Korea: Yŏngjo and the Politics of Sagacity, by JaHyun Kim Haboush 1988

COMPANIONS TO ASIAN STUDIES

Approaches to the Oriental Classics, ed. Wm. Theodore de Bary 1959
Early Chinese Literature, by Burton Watson. Also in paperback ed. 1962
Approaches to Asian Civilizations, ed. Wm. Theodore de Bary and Ainslie T. Embree 1964
The Classic Chinese Novel: A Critical Introduction, by C. T. Hsia. Also in paperback ed. 1968
Chinese Lyricism: Shih Poetry from the Second to the Twelfth Century, tr. Burton Watson. Also in paperback ed. 1971
A Syllabus of Indian Civilization, by Leonard A. Gordon and Barbara Stoler Miller 1971
Twentieth-Century Chinese Stories, ed. C. T. Hsia and Joseph S. M. Lau. Also in paperback ed. 1971
A Syllabus of Chinese Civilization, by J. Mason Gentzler, 2d ed. 1972
A Syllabus of Japanese Civilization, by H. Paul Varley, 2d ed. 1972
An Introduction to Chinese Civilization, ed. John Meskill, with the assistance of J. Mason Gentzler 1973
An Introduction to Japanese Civilization, ed. Arthur E. Tiedemann 1974
Ukifune: Love in the Tale of Genii, ed. Andrew Pekarik 1982
The Pleasures of Japanese Literature, by Donald Keene 1988
A Guide to Oriental Classics, ed. Wm. Theodore de Bary and Ainslie T. Embree; 3d edition ed. Amy Vladeck *Heinrich*, 2 vols. 1989

INTRODUCTION TO ASIAN CIVILIZATIONS

Wm. Theodore de Bary, General Editor

Sources of Japanese Tradition, 1958; paperback ed., 2 vols., 1964.2d ed., vol. 1, 2001, compiled by Wm. Theodore de Bary, Donald Keene, George Tanabe, and Paul Varley
Sources of Indian Tradition, 1958; paperback ed., 2 vols., 1964. 2d ed., 2 vols., 1988

Sources of Chinese Tradition, 1960, paperback ed., 2 vols., 1964.2d ed., vol. 1, 1999, compiled by Wm. Theodore de Bary and Irene Bloom; vol. 2, 2000, compiled by Wm. Theodore de Bary and Richard Lufrano

Sources of Korean Tradition, 1997; 2 vols., vol. 1, 1997, compiled by Peter H. Lee and Wm. Theodore de Bary; vol. 2, 2001, compiled by Yŏngjo Ch'oe, Peter H. Lee, and Wm. Theodore de Bary

NEO-CONFUCIAN STUDIES

Instructions for Practical Living and Other Neo-Confucian Writings by Wang Yang-ming, tr. Wing-tsit Chan 1963

Reflections.on Things at Hand: The Neo-Confucian Anthology, comp. Chu Hsi and Lii Tsu-ch'ien, tr. Wing-tsit Chan 1967

Self and Society in Ming Thought, by Wm. Theodore de Bary and the Conference on Ming Thought. Also in paperback ed. 1970

The Unfolding of Neo-Confucianism, by Wm. Theodore de Bary and the Conference on Seventeenth-Century Chinese Thought. Also in paperback ed. 1975

Pr.inciple and Practicality: Essays in Neo-Confucjanism and Practical Learning, ed. Wm. Theodore de Bary and Irene Bloom. Also in paperback ed. 1979

The Syncretic Religion of Lin Chao-en, by Judith A. Berling 1980

The Renewal of Buddhism in China: Chu.-hung and the Late Ming Synthesis, by Chiin-fang Yii 1981

Neo-Confucian Orthodoxy and the Learning of the Mind-and-Heart, by Win. Theodore de Bary 1981

Yiian Thought: Chinese Thought and Religio.n Under the Mongols, ed. Hok-lam Chan and Wm. Theodore de Bary 1982

The Liberal Tradition in China, by Wm. Theodore de Bary 1983

The Development and Decline of Chinese Cosmology, by John B. Henderson 1984

The Rise of Neo-Confucianism in Korea, by Wm. Theodore de Bary and JaHyun Kim Haboush 1985

Chiao Hung and th.e Restructuring of Neo-Confucinism in. Late Ming, by Edward T. Ch'ien 1985

Neo-Confucian Terms Explained: Pei-hsi tzu-i, by Ch'en Ch'un, ed. and trans. Wing-tsit Chan 1986

Knowledge Painfully Acquired: K'un-chih chi, by Lo Ch'in-shun, ed. and trans. Irene Bloom 1987

To Become a Sage: The Ten Diagrams on Sage Learning, by Yi T'oegye, ed. and trans. Michael C. Kalton 1988

The Message of the Mind in Neo-Confucian Thought, by Win. Theodore de Bary 1989